Perfect

Felicity Cloake is a journalist and food writer from London. She writes for the *Daily Mail*, the *Metro* and *Fire & Knives* magazine and has a weekly column in the *Guardian*. She was named Food Journalist of the Year and won the New Media of the Year Award at the 2011 Guild of Food Writers Awards. *Perfect* is her first book.

www.felicitycloake.com

Perfect

68 Essential Recipes for Every Cook's Repertoire

By

Felicity Cloake

FIG TREE
an imprint of
PENGUIN BOOKS

For all my *Guardian* Word of Mouth regulars:
I couldn't have done it without you

FIG TREE

Published by the Penguin Group
Penguin Books Ltd, 80 Strand, London WC2R ORL, England
Penguin Group (USA) Inc., 375 Hudson Street, New York, New York 10014, USA
Penguin Group (Canada), 90 Eglinton Avenue East, Suite 700, Toronto, Ontario, Canada M4P 2Y3
(a division of Pearson Penguin Canada Inc.)
Penguin Ireland, 25 St Stephen's Green, Dublin 2, Ireland (a division of Penguin Books Ltd)
Penguin Group (Australia), 250 Camberwell Road,
Camberwell, Victoria 3124, Australia (a division of Pearson Australia Group Pty Ltd)
Penguin Books India Pvt Ltd, 11 Community Centre,
Panchsheel Park, New Delhi – 110 017, India
Penguin Group (NZ), 67 Apollo Drive, Rosedale, Auckland 0632, New Zealand
(a division of Pearson New Zealand Ltd)
Penguin Books (South Africa) (Pty) Ltd, 24 Sturdee Avenue,
Rosebank, Johannesburg 2196, South Africa

Penguin Books Ltd, Registered Offices: 80 Strand, London WC2R ORL, England

www.penguin.com

First published 2011
1

Copyright © Felicity Cloake, 2011

Set in 12/14.75pt Mrs Eaves
Typeset by Palimpsest Book Production Limited,
Falkirk, Stirlingshire
Printed in Great Britain by Clays Ltd, St Ives plc

A CIP catalogue record for this book is available from the British Library

HARDBACK ISBN: 978–1–905–49083–7

www.greenpenguin.co.uk

MIX
Paper from
responsible sources
FSC
www.fsc.org   FSC™ C018179

Penguin Books is committed to a sustainable
future for our business, our readers and our
planet. This book is made from paper certified
by the Forest Stewardship Council.

Contents

Introduction

I remember my grandmother having one cookbook: a well-thumbed copy of *Mrs Beeton's Book of Household Management*, which, with its sections on servant management and General Observations on the Common Hog, held a special fascination for me. Presumably she had others — perhaps something from the *Good Housekeeping* stable, a booklet or two bearing the stamp of the Milk Marketing Board, maybe even a daringly modern Fanny Cradock — but if so, I never saw her using them.

Twenty years after Grandma's death, Mrs Beeton lives with me. She sits in splendour alongside Elizabeth David and Jane Grigson in my paperback section — one of eight shelves given over to gluttony. I've got a whole row devoted to Italian cookery, the entire works of Nigel Slater, books on everything from venison to vegetarianism, and a binder stuffed with tatty recipes I've torn out of magazines and never made (when exactly is the right time and place for a kedgeree Scotch egg?).

The choice is bewildering — how on earth can I hope to make anything when even something as simple as a scone throws up so much conflicting advice? Cookery is not always an exact science, but after all these years, you'd think we could at least agree on the best way to make a loaf of bread. Hence my column in the *Guardian*, which since January 2010 has seen me pitting expert against expert and emerging triumphant from the fray, clutching a single perfect recipe. Along the way it's thrown up some shocks (Delia Smith's unorthodox approach to pastry making springs to mind) and confirmed a fair few long-held suspicions (Simon Hopkinson and Lindsey Bareham can do no wrong, while Gordon Ramsay cooks as if he's got a kitchen brigade behind him), but I hope it's ironed out a few mysteries as well, so all that washing up hasn't been in vain.

What follows is a collection of some of my favourite recipes, distilled from the collected wisdom of some of our best-loved chefs and cookery writers. And this time, they really will work. Cooking is like anything in life – it helps to be prepared. I won't claim that if you cook your way through this book you'll be ready to welcome the Michelin inspectors into your dining room, but I reckon you'd probably stand a fair chance on *Masterchef*. Get the basics right, learn how to make a decent stew, bake a great sponge, or mix up some mayonnaise, and the kitchen is your oyster – on your culinary CV, these are all eminently transferable skills. M. F. K. Fisher, probably the finest food writer America has ever produced, notes in her essay collection *An Alphabet for Gourmets* that 'gastronomical precepts', as she calls them, must, for the most part, be followed before they can be broken. She can do things with five ingredients that French masterchef Escoffier 'perhaps never dreamed of', she says, but in order to do them well, she must follow the basic rules for stock making, poaching, etcetera set down by such culinary masters.

Just as homemade stock opens up a hundred delicious possibilities, from risotto to soup, knowing how to make a hollandaise will equip you to whip up eggs Benedict and give asparagus the respect it deserves, as well as creating any number of fancy-sounding spin-off sauces. With these skills in your armoury, you're finally ready to do battle with the celebrity chefs.

MY KITCHEN

You don't need cupboards full of equipment to cook – certain gadgets will make life easier, but, as I try to remember whenever I'm pounding a pesto with gritted teeth and aching arms, most of these recipes were around long before John Lewis, so there's very little that can't be achieved with a generous dollop of determination. Strong arms will definitely help, of course; who needs the gym when there's mayonnaise to make?

Basics

These are things which every kitchen should have. It makes sense to spend more on better-quality knives and pans, which will last you years, and make a real difference to your cooking, and save on things like crockery and cutlery, which can always be upgraded later. (As Len Deighton points out in *French Cooking for Men*, if in doubt, always opt for the boring-looking professional sort, rather than the 'bright coloured one with the dodgy-looking plastic handle'.) It's also worth splashing out on Microplane graters; they may be a bit more expensive than the traditional sort, but they make zesting a doddle, and can reduce even the most mature Parmesan to feather-light clouds of flavour.

- 1 good chef's knife and sharpener (a knife wheel, which you just need to run your knife through a couple of times on a regular basis, is the easiest choice for beginners)

- Two chopping boards (wooden is the best for knives, and will last longest if you look after it well — never leave it to soak, or put it in the dishwasher)

- Heavy-duty scissors

- Potato masher

- Tongs — trust me, to paraphrase Masterchef's John Torode, these will change your life; choose a silicone version if you use non-stick pans

- Silicone spatula for getting every last bit of cake mix out of the bowl, or soup out of the pan

- Metal or plastic fish slice

- Wooden spoon

- Balloon whisk

- Slotted spoon

- Ladle

- Box grater

- Vegetable peeler

- Large metal or plastic spoon

- Large heavy-based frying pan, with lid
- Small, medium and large heavy-based saucepans, all with lids

- Cast-iron casserole (for use on the hob and in the oven)

- Baking tray
- Heavy-based roasting tin
- Muffin tin

- Loaf tin
- Tart tin
- Cooling rack

- Tin opener
- Corkscrew and bottle opener

- Measuring jug
- Electronic scales

- Colander
- Fine sieve
- Large mixing bowl

- Rolling pin
- Pyrex bowl that fits over one of the saucepans to make a bain-marie

- Pestle and mortar

Useful, but not essential

- Small heavy-based frying pan
- Baking dishes — if they're presentable enough to go from oven to table, it will save on washing up; I like the classic blue and white enamel ones, which also have the benefit of being pleasingly cheap
- Cast-iron griddle pan
- Ruler or tape measure
- Measuring spoons
- Steamer
- Stockpot
- Fine and coarse Microplane graters
- Citrus reamer for juicing lemons and limes
- Food processor
- Electric stick blender and whisk
- Food mixer
- Gravy separator
- Baking beans
- Pastry brush
- Electronic thermometer
- Pan whisk
- Roasting rack
- Carving knife and fork
- Meat cleaver
- Boning, bread and kitchen knives

Sharpen your knives after every use, and dry them immediately after washing to prevent them corroding. It's worth investing in a knife skills course, or book (I've got Marianne Lumb's *Kitchen Knife Skills)* to hone your technique — you'll save both time and fingers in the long run, and, in the short term, get to show off a bit.

Pantry

Once you build up a good store cupboard, you'll find you not only spend relatively little on ingredients, but will also always have something in the cupboard for a good meal: no more late-night cereals, or ill-advised 2 a.m. takeaway orders. Well, that's the theory, anyway. You don't have to buy all these ingredients at once, but if you're cooking regularly, you'll find you need most of them before long.

- *Plain flour*

- *Instant yeast*

- *Cornflour*

- *Oats*

- *Baking powder*

- *Bicarbonate of soda*

- *Caster sugar*

- Light brown sugar

- Icing sugar

- Vanilla pods or vanilla extract

- Cocoa

- Dried fruit: raisins, currants, etc.

- Pine nuts

- Blanched and flaked almonds

- Walnuts

- Hazelnuts

- English mustard powder

- Dijon mustard

- White and red wine vinegar

- Olive oil

- Vegetable or groundnut oil

- Soy sauce

- Marmite or Bovril (to beef up sauces as well as for eating on toast)

- Ketchup

- Worcestershire sauce

- Hot sauce (e.g. Tabasco)

- Fish sauce

- Coconut milk, tinned

- Anchovies

- Capers

- Dried herbs and spices; you'll collect these as you go
  along, but these are the ones I use most often: chilli
  powder, whole nutmeg, coriander and cumin seeds,
  smoked paprika, thyme, bay leaves, cinnamon

- Honey

- Sea salt — fine for cooking, flaked for finishing dishes

- Black pepper

- Good-quality stock cubes: vegetable, chicken and beef

- Basmati rice

- Risotto rice

- Rice or egg noodles

- Couscous

- Dried pasta: one long, one shaped

- Chickpeas, lentils, beans — either dried or tinned

- Tinned tomatoes

- Tomato purée

- White and red wine, for cooking

Fresh and frozen ingredients
These are things it's always useful to have around.

- *Milk*

- *Butter*

- *Crème fraîche*

- *Cheddar and Parmesan cheese*

- *Bread*

- *Garlic*

- *Onions*

- *Potatoes*

- *Living herbs (I've found rosemary, thyme, parsley, mint, bay and chives are all relatively easy to keep alive)*

- Homemade stock

- Frozen breadcrumbs

- Vanilla ice cream

- Frozen seafood and white fish fillets

- Frozen peas and beans

- Frozen berries

- Frozen puff and shortcrust pastry — either homemade or shop-bought

- Frozen egg whites — the Two Chicks fresh brand is widely available, and can be kept in the freezer for up to 2 years

CHAPTER 1

Eggs and Cheese

*E*ggs are nothing less than a culinary miracle – the surprising gift of bird to man. Handily packaged, extraordinarily versatile, and utterly delicious, they should be one of the first things anyone learns to cook. Delia, who has made a great deal of money from teaching the nation how to boil an egg (and good for her – we certainly needed it), is an authority on the subject, but there's no substitute for experimentation. After all, even the best eggs won't set you back much more than a couple of pounds per half dozen, and within that box is boundless potential, from the simple delights of a fried egg sandwich to the more rarefied pleasures of the rich and wobbling quiche – there really is no excuse for not being able to do them justice. Remember, it's what the poultry would have wanted. Probably.

Perfect
Boiled Eggs

*B*oiled eggs aren't just for plonking under sweetly knitted cosies and serving with soldiers – though, paired with the brown bread on page 189, they're hard to beat. They're also the ultimate neatly packaged picnic food, and, soft-boiled and broken over a pile of steamed asparagus or sprouting broccoli spears, they elevate simplicity to an art form.

You'd think the clue to cooking them was in the name, but think again. Canadian foodie Susan Sampson claims, in her otherwise very useful book *12,167 Kitchen and Cooking Secrets*, that boiling is the worst thing you can do to an egg – instead, after bringing the water to the barest simmer, she likes to steep them off the heat. After peeling three hard-boiled eggs in succession that quickly reveal themselves to be all but raw, I crossly conclude that Susan must have kept one particular secret to herself.

She's right about not boiling them, though; Rose Prince, food writer and author of *The New English Kitchen*, starts her hard-boiled eggs off in cold water, on the basis that prolonged exposure to heat makes the whites rubbery, and after experimenting, I'm inclined to agree – soft-boiled seem to be fine dropped gently straight into a pan of boiling water (use a slotted spoon to avoid cracking them), but after about 5 minutes the whites become distinctly tough. Len Deighton, author of a wildly successful series of 'cookstrip' cartoons, as well as *The Ipcress File* and much other espionage literature, helpfully points out in *French Cooking for Men* that the Gallic word *frémir*, or shiver, perfectly describes the correct way to cook eggs.

Putting eggs into cold rather than hot water also makes them less likely to crack — and it's important not to overcrowd the pan for this reason, so they don't bump into each other during cooking. Once they're done, take the eggs straight out of the pan and run them under cold water for a couple of minutes; this will arrest the cooking process and allow you to peel them more quickly. To begin peeling the shell, rap the wide end sharply on a hard surface — rolling them on the counter may be satisfying, but you're more likely to end up picking splinters of shell out of the white.

Soft-boiled (just firm white, liquid yolk): Lower the eggs into boiling water and cook for 4 minutes

Medium-boiled (firm white, half-liquid yolk): Put the egg into cold water and bring to the boil, then turn the heat down and simmer for 5 minutes

Hard-boiled (firm white, firm, sliceable yolk): Put the egg into cold water and bring to the boil, then turn the heat down and simmer for 7½ minutes

----

How to judge the freshness of an egg

Drop it gently into a bowl of cold water. If it sinks, it's very fresh, if it hovers on one end, then it's older but still edible, and if it floats, chuck it very gently in the bin — it's likely to be rotten. Interestingly, although fresher eggs make more stable meringues, and are easier to poach, as they have a firmer structure, very fresh eggs are a nightmare to peel, so don't use them for hard-boiling.

Perfect
Fried Eggs

*I*t's the star attraction of one of our most famous national dishes, yet fried eggs are still massacred by the great British caff on a daily basis — as a quick flick through Russell M. Davies' masterwork, *Egg Bacon Chips & Beans* (a survey of British caffs through the medium of his favourite order), indicates. A good fried egg is not as simple as it sounds. The whites should be firm and flavourful, yet still creamy, while the yolk should be just set, ready to spill at the merest caress of a knife. If there are people who savour the brittle lace of an overcooked white, this can only be through long and miserable habit.

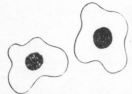 Setting the white without spoiling the yolk is a precarious science, however. The notoriously perfectionist French chef Bernard Loiseau, who, haunted by the fear of losing his third Michelin star, took his own life in 2003, solved the problem by cooking them separately, in saucers of butter set in a pan of simmering water, and then sliding the cooked yolk back on to the white to serve. All well and good, monsieur, but it's pretty fiddly, and almost impossible to do in quantity. Also, it is *definitely* cheating.

A friend scornfully suggests I'm making too much of the issue: have I never heard of basting the white with hot fat during cooking? Not only is this process labour-intensive, causing me to burn the toast, but it doesn't really work: however hard I try, I'm still left with a ring of pale jelly around the carefully unsplashed yolk. The online food forum *chowhound.com* (hours of fun) suggests filling the pan with just enough fat to cover the white, but, of course, as well as effectively deep-frying most of the egg, this overcooks the bottom of the yolk.

The solution is much simpler – in this method, adopted from the great Lyonnais chef Fernand Point, the egg is fried, ever so gently, in warm butter. After playing around with timings for a bit, I hit upon the idea of covering it while it cooks, so it simultaneously steams and fries, which, if I say so myself, is pure genius, and absolutely foolproof. Point suggests drizzling the butter over the cooked egg before serving, but he was immensely fat and died before the age of sixty, so you might want to skip that part. The fresher the egg, by the way, the better the white will hold together in the pan.

Serves 1

1 large free-range egg
A generous knob of butter
Salt and pepper

1. Crack your egg into a saucer, and heat the butter in a heavy-based frying pan over a low heat. Have ready a saucepan lid – ideally one that is slightly too small for the pan, so you can wedge it inside, just above the egg.
2. When the butter has melted fully, swirl the pan to coat, then slide in the egg; it should not sizzle as it hits the fat. Cover with a lid and leave for 2½ minutes, then check on it every 30 seconds – when it's done to your liking, lift it out with a slotted spoon, season gently, and serve.

Perfect
Scrambled Eggs

*N*othing brings on a bad mood quicker than bad scrambled eggs. Equally, not much beats the lazy, luxurious pleasure of well-cooked ones, but unless you breakfast regularly in smart hotels, they're something best left to slow weekend mornings at home — scrambled eggs can't be hurried, although making them in a bain-marie, in the traditional French fashion, isn't worth the extra washing up, or the forty-five minutes you'll never get back.

Neither can they be bullied — don't whisk the eggs together as the godfather of modern French cookery, the great Escoffier, did before adding them to a hot pan, and don't add cream to the mixture in imitation of  Australian celebrity chef Bill Granger's famous scrambled eggs: overworking eggs makes them tough, and too much dairy masks their rich flavour. Instead, take a leaf out of Gordon Ramsay's book and crack the eggs straight into a cold pan, saving on washing up and making life easier for yourself in the process.

Gordon hasn't quite hit the egg jackpot, though; unless you like to start the day with an eggy purée, I'd avoid his way of furiously stirring them into submission — adopt Bill's more laid-back approach, and you'll end up with large, creamy curds which have a much more interesting texture — and look a damn sight more appetizing too. I don't think Ramsay's right that adding salt during

cooking will ruin the texture either; it's essential for flavour.
Sprinkle it on at the table, and you'll need a lot more to get the same
effect.

The eggs will carry on cooking in their own heat after leaving the
pan, so it's important to add some cold fat at the end to arrest this
process, or you'll be sitting down to overdone eggs for all your
pains. A knob of butter, as suggested by Delia, is good for everyday
eggs, but if you're feeling luxurious, a dollop of Gordon's crème
fraîche finishes them off perfectly, adding a deliciously subtle
tanginess to proceedings – all you need is a slice of toasted
sourdough and a few chives for the perfect Saturday morning
breakfast.

Scrambled eggs aren't diet food – a poached version, as advocated by
one *New York Times* writer, whisked together and decanted into
simmering water, may be free from butter, crème fraîche and the
like, but rubbery, watery and with a distinct whiff of space food
about them, they sure hide their virtues under a bushel. No, great
scrambled eggs require a generous hand with the dairy and single-
minded devotion to stirring and watching – leave them alone for a
second, and they'll overcook. Get someone else to make the toast.

Serves 1

2 large free-range eggs
A knob of butter
A pinch of salt
1 teaspoon crème fraîche

1. Break the eggs into a small, heavy-based frying pan or saucepan and add the butter and salt. Place over a medium-high heat, and stir the eggs together with a wooden spoon.
2. Once well combined, leave the eggs for 10 seconds, then stir again. If they're setting too quickly, take them off the heat to stir and then replace. Repeat until they begin to set, then stir continuously until they're nearly as cooked as you like them; always take them off the heat before they're done.
3. Whip the pan off the heat, stir in the crème fraîche, and serve immediately.

Good things to mix into scrambled eggs, from around the world, in no particular order

Britain: Wild garlic; chopped steamed asparagus; ham and spring onions; crumbled black pudding; flaked smoked mackerel or hot smoked salmon; crab and chives; steamed and squeezed spinach with Lancashire cheese

Spain: Cooked and sliced chorizo and green Padrón peppers

Italy: Tomato, basil and Parmesan

Turkey: Onions, peppers, tomatoes and chillies with mint and crumbled feta (*menemen*)

Mexico: Onion, tomato, coriander and green chillies (*huevos a la Mexicana*)

India: Onion, garlic, chillies, fresh ginger, tomato and coriander (*akoori*)

China: Spring onions, soy sauce and prawns

Perfect
Poached Eggs

*P*oached eggs are the aristocrat of the breakfast table – a subtler pleasure than your workaday fried numbers, more luxurious than a safe soft-boiled egg, they're notoriously temperamental, making them a high-days and holidays treat for many. Crack their secret, however, and you can eat them every morning if you so desire.

Despite experimenting with the heat-and-leave methods favoured by Margaret Costa, the post-war cookery writer who deserves to be just as well known as her contemporary Elizabeth David, and Delia Smith, I reckon you can't make a proper poached egg without a vortex. After cracking numerous eggs into barely simmering water and allowing them to gently steep there until cooked, I remain convinced that a whirlpool is necessary if you're to end up with a well-shaped egg, rather than something that looks like it's come out of the pick and mix. It's the pressure of the water that pushes the egg in on itself; put it into still water and it will spread out as flat as a pancake.

Mark the words of Ramsay protégé Marcus Wareing, who learnt to poach eggs at the feet of the breakfast chef at the Savoy, and whisk your pan of boiling water vigorously, pause for a second, then gently slide the egg into the centre, turn down the heat and leave for 3 minutes. (Breaking it into a small jug or bowl makes this a lot easier – you don't want to be fiddling around with bits of shell at this crucial point in proceedings.) As chef and restaurateur Mark Hix points out, the deeper the vessel, the more teardrop-shaped the result, so use a saucepan rather than a frying pan. In an ideal world you'd only ever be called upon to poach spanking fresh eggs, but in reality, adding a drop of vinegar to the white helps to keep the egg together without imparting the overpoweringly acidic flavour that often results from tipping a capful into the water.

If I'm poaching a few eggs simultaneously, *Telegraph* food writer Rose Prince's clingfilm trick is unbelievably useful: crack the egg into a ramekin lined with lightly greased clingfilm, twist together the ends to seal, then lift the package out (it should resemble a goldfish at the fair) and dunk it into simmering water. The eggs don't have the perfect beauty of those cooked by the method below, but it does make life easier if they aren't absolutely fresh.

Poached eggs are a key ingredient in eggs Benedict (see page 145 for the hollandaise recipe), but they're also delicious on salads, with corned beef hash and smoked fish, and in soupy Japanese ramen dishes.

1 large fresh free-range egg
1 drop of malt or white wine vinegar

1. Half fill a medium saucepan with water and bring to the boil. Meanwhile, crack the egg into a small jug or bowl and add a drop of vinegar.
2. Stir the boiling water vigorously with a balloon whisk until you have a whirlpool, then immediately slip the egg into the centre, lowering the jug a couple of centimetres into the water.
3. Turn the heat down low and cook for 3 minutes — use a timer to prevent overcooking.

4. Drain the egg on kitchen paper, and serve immediately. If you're poaching it in advance, drop it straight into a bowl of iced water instead, or it will carry on cooking; to reheat, simply warm the egg through in a pan of gently simmering water.

How to store eggs
Eggs should be stored at a constant temperature — it's not necessary to keep them refrigerated, except in midsummer, but they will keep longer in the cold. Bear in mind that eggshells are extremely porous, and will absorb the smell of anything you keep them near — this is useful if you happen to come into a truffle, but less so if you store them near some fish or strong cheese, so keep them in their box. Eggs should always be stored with the pointy end downwards; this keeps the air pocket at the top, which slows down the ageing process.

Perfect
Cheese Soufflé

*I*f you believe the hype, soufflés are temperamental little things,
liable to spectacular collapse if you so much as hiccough in their
presence – the stuff of masterchefs. In fact, there's not much more
to them than your average cake; they're simply a savoury or sweet
base enriched with egg yolks and then lightened with an egg-white
foam. The air bubbles in the foam expand dramatically in the heat
of the oven, causing the soufflé to rise – and then, of course, shrink
again in the cold of the room, which accounts for the dish's
celebrated tendency to collapse. There's really no more mystery to it
than that. As Harold McGee, the scientifically minded food writer
championed by Heston Blumenthal, points out, as long as you
manage to get some air into the mixture to begin with, your soufflés
will rise during cooking: it's a law of nature. (Sadly, of course, they
will eventually also fall.)

The question, then, is not how to get them to rise in the first
place, but how to achieve maximum height, and keep them
that way for as long as possible. I try adding extra egg
whites, as suggested in Darina Allen's *Ballymaloe Cookery
Course*, but although the rise is significantly more
impressive, the flavour isn't as good; egg whites and
air being, of course, largely tasteless. Folding the base
and egg whites together slowly and gently, as suggested by McGee in
contradiction to the general instruction to do so as quickly as possible,
does seem to result in less air loss, and his tip about cooking them in a

bain-marie to 'moderate' the bottom oven temperature is also a good one; the soufflé seems creamier somehow.

Most recipes suggest running a finger around the inside rim of the mixture before cooking, to create a neat 'top hat' effect in the oven, rather than the exploding cauliflower effect which plagues the amateur soufflé chef. This does work, if you do it straight before you put it into the oven, but I quite like the more eccentric look myself.

The higher the oven temperature, the higher the soufflé will rise, and the more spectacularly it will fall – but after some disappointing results between 160°C, as used by Launceston Place chef Tristan Welch, and 180°C, as in Raymond Blanc's recipe, I happen upon Xanthe Clay in the *Telegraph*, who blasts the soufflés at 220°C. They're boldly brown on top and still wonderfully quivery inside – and her heavy hand with the cheese (she carelessly pops in twice as much as Darina Allen) yields delicious results. More cheese is, as usual, a very good thing. However, I decide to turn the heat down slightly to 200°C, so they aren't quite as dry on top.

Coating the inside of the ramekins with breadcrumbs, as suggested by *Leiths Cookery Bible*, apparently does nothing to help the soufflé to rise, as is popularly supposed, but it does provide a pleasing textural contrast to the egg. I also take a tip from Margaret Costa's *Four Seasons Cookery Book* and keep some of that lovely cheese back until the last minute, so it doesn't quite have time to melt into the sauce; as she observes, it's a real treat to encounter a string of Gruyère when you dig in with your spoon.

Good luck – and remember, you can slam doors, dance around, and even open the oven during cooking if you like; as long as the oven's hot, they'll still rise, I promise. Go on, be bold, give it a try.

Makes 6

40g butter, plus 20g melted butter for greasing the ramekins
40g plain flour
300ml whole milk
20g white breadcrumbs
4 large free-range eggs
½ teaspoon English mustard powder
100g Gruyère, finely grated
50g Parmesan, finely grated
Salt and pepper

1. Preheat the oven to 200°C/400°F/gas 6. Melt the butter in a small pan and stir in the flour. Cook, stirring, for a couple of minutes, then gradually whisk in the milk until smooth, and heat gently until the mixture comes to the boil. Simmer for 5 minutes, stirring until thickened but still pourable, then transfer to a large bowl and set aside to cool slightly.

2. Meanwhile, brush six ramekins or small ovenproof dishes or cups with the melted butter, using upward strokes, and coat with breadcrumbs. Separate the eggs, putting the whites into a large clean bowl (not a plastic one). Half fill a roasting tin with just-boiled water from the kettle, and put into the oven.

3. Stir the mustard powder, 75g of the Gruyère and all the Parmesan into the sauce until smooth, and then stir in the egg yolks one by one. Finally, add the rest of the cheese, season and give one brief stir to mix.

4. Whisk the egg whites with a pinch of salt until stiff, but still moist and glossy (beware of over-whipping them: they shouldn't look dry or grainy), and stir a couple of tablespoons into the cheese base. Then very slowly and gently fold in the rest with a spatula.

Divide the mixture between the ramekins and level the top with a palette knife.

5. Run your thumb inside the rim of each ramekin to create a groove in the mixture, then immediately put the ramekins into the roasting tin of water and cook for about 12 minutes, until they are golden and well risen. Serve immediately, before they shrink!

A soufflé for all seasons
Once you've mastered a basic cheese soufflé, you'll be empowered to experiment with other flavours: chopped ham and chives, sautéd spinach, leeks or mushrooms, crumbled goat's cheese and thyme — fold the extra ingredients through at the same point as the cheese in the recipe above. A classic addition is smoked haddock, cooked in milk and then broken into flakes — the milk is then used to make the soufflé base. Sweet soufflés work on the same principle, but usually start with a pastry cream, flavoured with chocolate, coffee or fruit purée.

For something so delicate, soufflés freeze surprisingly well. Freeze the ramekins as soon as you've filled them, and simply allow an extra 5 minutes in the oven.

Perfect
Spanish Omelette

*T*here are few things in life that aren't improved by the addition of potato — and the Spanish omelette is a perfect example; comfort food par excellence, which transforms a couple of humble ingredients into a dish fit for *el rey* himself.

Simple is best where the *tortilla de patatas* is concerned: in its homeland, even the inclusion of onion is a matter of serious controversy. Heresy or not, I reckon that, sweated down to melting softness beforehand, and slightly caramelized as recommended by former Brindisa chef José Pizarro, it adds a beautiful sweetness to the dish. Make the most of this by putting the cooked onion and potatoes into the egg mixture to infuse for 10 minutes before cooking. If you like a light and fluffy omelette then separate your eggs, and whisk the whites into a foam before folding them into the mixture just before cooking — personally, I think this variation gives height at the expense of flavour.

Ferran Adrià, the so-called 'dean of molecular gastronomy', whose ground-breaking Catalonian restaurant, El Bulli, was five times named the best in the world, finishes his omelette under the grill (he also uses crisps; we'll gloss over that particular experiment), but I think it gives a dryer, more caramelized result that I'm not particularly keen on. If you're possessed of a shaky hand, however, it's easier than flipping it. You can also buy special tortilla-flipping tools, or *gira tortillas*, online, but unless you're going into large-scale production, a plate or saucepan lid will do just as well.

Opinions vary as to how long you should cook a true Spanish omelette – some devotees like a liquid centre, held together by the thinnest of skins, but as long as you don't cook it until it's absolutely dry and solid, it's a matter of personal preference: I like mine slightly creamy towards the middle.

A good Spanish omelette really hinges on the quality of the potatoes – get waxy ones, so they don't fall apart, and cook them low and slow in plenty of olive oil until silky soft. Don't be tempted to cut down on the oil – it will lack richness. Once you've got the basics right, you can play around with this recipe, adding shredded Serrano ham, or cooked piquillo peppers, or smoked paprika as you fancy – although if you're serving it to a Spaniard, you're probably better off calling it a frittata.

Serves 4 as a main or 8 as a tapa

    300ml olive oil
    1 medium onion, finely diced
    750g waxy potatoes such as Jersey Royals
       or Charlottes, peeled and cut into
       thin slices (like thick crisps)
    5 medium free-range eggs, beaten
    Salt and pepper
    2 tablespoons extra virgin olive oil

1. Heat the olive oil in a large frying pan (26cm diameter would be ideal) over a medium flame, add the onion and cook gently for 20 minutes, until soft and brown. Rinse the potato slices under cold running water and pat dry with kitchen paper. Add the potatoes to the onions and cook, stirring frequently, for about 15 minutes, until the potatoes are on the point of falling apart. Drain the potatoes in a colander set over a bowl. Keep the oil for your next omelette; you should have at least a third of it left, but don't use it more than three times.

2. Beat the eggs in a medium bowl and add the drained potatoes and onions. Season, and leave to stand for 10 minutes.

3. Put a smaller frying pan (18cm would be ideal, and preferably non-stick) over a medium heat and add the extra virgin olive oil. Turn to coat, then add the mixture – it should almost fill the pan. Cook for about 12 minutes, until it comes away from the edge of the pan and there is only a thin layer of liquid egg on the top. Loosen the tortilla all the way round with a palette knife.

4. Place a plate, or a saucepan lid, over the pan, and invert it so the tortilla flips on to the plate. Slide it back into the pan so the cooked base is now on top, tipping any liquid egg in with it. Cook until it is springy to the touch – about 3 minutes more for a slightly softer centre, and 5 for a more solid result. Be careful not to overcook it: it should still be moist in the middle, even if you prefer it cooked through. Allow to cool slightly before serving.

TIP

How to separate eggs

You don't need a special
gadget to separate eggs — in
fact, the best tool is right
in front of you. Break the egg
into your outstretched hand and
allow the white to run through your
fingers, while the yolk stays snugly on
top. If you need to whip up the whites, however, use
the eggshell instead, as your skin will give off grease
that may prevent them forming a proper foam —
toss the yolk from one half shell to the other, while
allowing the white to fall into a bowl below.

Perfect
Omelettes

*T*here is something magical about a good omelette — the way a couple of eggs and a pinch of salt can, in less than a minute, achieve such greatness. Light yet rich in flavour, swift but satisfying, the omelette is the ultimate frugal supper. As with all very simple things, the omelette has attracted a certain mystique amongst those convinced that there must be more to it than meets the eye. In the titular essay from the collected short works of Elizabeth David, *An Omelette and a Glass of Wine*, the famously ferocious 'awful genius' of post-war food writing, who introduced a whole generation to the joys of continental cookery, tells of a certain Madame Poulard, celebrated throughout France for her omelettes.

The gourmands of France slavered over her light and fluffy creations, and indulged themselves with endless speculation as to her secret — water, foie gras, a special breed of hen, all were held responsible for these works of genius. Finally, David writes, someone saw fit to ask Madame herself for her recipe. 'I break some good eggs in a bowl, I beat them well, I put a good piece of butter in the pan. I throw the eggs into it and I shake it constantly. I am happy, monsieur, if this recipe pleases you.'

Before we start, let's clarify that the omelette of which I speak here is a classical French-style one, a rich cigar of fluffy deliciousness, rather than a dense yellow half moon oozing cheese and ham. You can guess how to make those yourself, there's not much skill involved. This sort, however, aspires to delicacy, and height – and that's more difficult to achieve.

The classic French culinary encyclopedia *Larousse Gastronomique* adds milk to its recipe, and Darina Allen at Ballymaloe Cookery School suggests a couple of tablespoons of water, both ingredients which make the omelette fluffier, but which, in my opinion, dilute its rich eggy flavour. Really, you just need eggs (at room temperature or they'll take too long to set) and butter – not only does it impart flavour, but, unlike oil, butter helpfully foams when the pan is hot enough to add the eggs (that pan, by the way, should be heavy, and tailored to the size of your omelette – 23cm is ideal for one person. Le Creuset make a perfect cast-iron example which is well worth the investment if you eat them a lot). *Larousse* also helpfully suggests that, for a really spectacular omelette, you should whisk your yolks and whites separately, and fold them together before serving – but although the result is impressive, it lacks the deep flavour of a real omelette. Style over substance.

Purists such as Julia Child insist that stirring your omelette with a spatula will ruin the texture, but she must have had wrists of steel to flip her pan so dextrously – if Michel Roux Jr, Marcus Wareing and Ballymaloe Cookery School all allow it, then it's good enough for me.

For a great omelette, you need three things: good ingredients (and plenty of them, in the case of the butter), the right-sized pan, and fearlessly quick wits. Time is of the essence – it should be on a plate within a minute.

Serves 1

2 large free-range eggs
Salt and pepper
The filling of your choice (optional, but
    Parmesan, Gruyère, tomatoes, fresh herbs,
    ham, smoked fish and sautéd mushrooms
    are all favourites of mine)
A generous knob of butter (about a tablespoon)

1. Whisk together the eggs until just mixed, then season. Lay out any fillings you are using by the hob.

2. Heat a 23cm pan over a medium-high flame, add the butter and swirl to coat. When the foam begins to die down, pour in the eggs. They should sizzle.

3. Shake the pan to distribute the eggs evenly, then leave for 20 seconds, until they begin to bubble. Add any filling.

4. Using a spatula or fork, draw in the sides of the eggs to the centre while shaking the pan to redistribute the liquid to the edges. The omelette is done when still slightly runny in the middle.

5. Take off the heat, and fold two edges into the middle. Shake the pan so they roll together, then tilt it and turn your omelette on to a warm plate (you can tidy it up before serving if you like). Season and eat immediately!

Egg guide

Although hens are the go-to egg producers in this country, they don't have a monopoly on the business. Here, from the smallest to the most mighty, are the different kinds you might come across:

Quail's eggs: Laid by the most diminutive of game birds, these prettily speckled eggs are about the size of a large stuffed olive, and have a higher proportion of yolk to white than a hen's egg. You can fry them and use them as a rather comical-looking garnish, but I like to soft boil them and serve with celery salt as a nibble. Simmer for 2 minutes, cool in iced water, then peel — or better still, get people to peel their own; they can be fiddly little things.

Gull's eggs: These have a very short season from mid-April to mid-May and, as they must be collected from wild birds, tend to be expensive — you're more likely to find them on a restaurant menu than at the supermarket. They have a rich, slightly minerally flavour, and can be treated in much the same way as a quail's egg.

Duck eggs: Slightly larger than hen's eggs, and higher in fat, they have a rich creamy flavour, and produce fluffier results when used in baking. Lovely soft-boiled too.

Goose eggs: Twice as large as a duck egg, these share their rich flavour and dense, translucent whites, which can turn rubbery at high heats. Better scrambled or soft-boiled than fried. Generally only available in spring and summer.

Ostrich eggs: If you come across one of these, bear in mind that it's the equivalent of 24 hen's eggs — and that you will need to boil it for an hour, and cut into the shell with a hacksaw, by which point the novelty will probably have worn off. You can, of course, also pierce a hole in the bottom, empty out the bottom to scramble, and decorate the shell instead.

Perfect
Quiche

*H*urrah for the prohibition on real men eating quiche – all the more for the rest of us. This classic French pastry has been done a major disservice by mass production: the flabby black sheep of the supermarket picnic basket bears little resemblance to the delicately wobbling, full-flavoured beauties you can turn out at home. (Elizabeth David is characteristically waspish on the subject in her essay 'Your Perfected Hostess'.) A quiche is essentially a rich baked custard, encased in crisp savoury pastry – and what's not to like about that?

Larousse Gastronomique informs me that, although quiche was made with bread dough in days of yore, both shortcrust and puff are now quite acceptable substitutes. Shortcrust is the classic in this country, but after experimenting with *Guardian* baker Dan Lepard's classic quiche, with its delectable flaky pastry, I realize the quiche's creamy filling is crying out for a bit of crunch. Rough puff it is – in their culinary survey of post-war Britain, *The Prawn Cocktail Years*, Simon Hopkinson and Lindsey Bareham suggest brushing the base with a little beaten egg to help seal it, which is helpful; a soggy bottom has been the ruination of many a picnic.

The filling should be generously eggy, rather than blandly creamy – I find *Good Food* magazine's ultimate quiche recipe, with its generous helpings of double cream and crème fraîche, rather insipid; the Elizabeth David version, which contains a greater proportion of egg, is much firmer and richer in flavour. The winner, however, is California's Thomas Keller, whose silky custard is so light it almost melts in the mouth, thanks to some vigorous whisking of the mixture before cooking. Keller is adamant that to be worthy of the name, a quiche must be made in a deep pan — you need something at least 3cm tall for a smooth, rich texture.

Adding the ingredients in stages helps to distribute them more evenly throughout the quiche, so you don't have to dig deep. One of the nice things about quiches is that you can add pretty much any ingredient you happen to have lying about — smoked bacon is the thing for the classic Quiche Lorraine, but I also like leek, goat's cheese and spinach, cheese and caramelized onion, spinach and salmon . . . the important thing is to ensure whatever it is won't leak any water into the filling. This means sautéing onions, leeks and bacon, and blanching and squeezing out leafy vegetables such as spinach.

Refrigeration will spoil the pastry, so eat this up as quickly as possible — but keep away from real men; they might forget themselves.

Serves 6

1 quantity of rough puff pastry (see page 187), rolled out on a floured surface

4 large free-range eggs and 2 egg
   yolks (keep 1 egg white for brushing
   the pastry)
200g dry cure smoked streaky
   bacon, chopped
320ml double cream
Salt

1. Preheat the oven to 180°C/350°F/gas 4. Grease a deep (at least
   3cm) 20cm fluted tart tin, and line it with the pastry, leaving an
   extra few centimetres of overhang to minimize shrinkage. Keep
   any extra in case you need it for remedial work later. Line with
   foil (shiny-side down) and weight down with baking beans or
   rice. Place on a baking tray and blind bake in the oven for 40
   minutes, then remove the foil and beans and patch up any holes
   with the extra pastry if necessary. Brush the base with egg white
   and put back into the oven for 10 minutes. Carefully trim the
   overhanging pastry to neaten.
2. Heat a small pan and cook the bacon for 8–10 minutes, until
   cooked through, but not crisp. Drain and spread half over the
   hot base.
3. Put the cream and the eggs and yolks into a large bowl (or a
   food mixer if you have one) with ¼ teaspoon of salt, and beat
   together slowly until combined, then give it a fast whisk for 30
   seconds until frothy. Pour over the base to fill and then sprinkle
   over the rest of the bacon. Bake for 20 minutes and then keep
   an eye on it – it's done when it's puffed up, but still wobbly at
   the centre. Allow to cool slightly before serving – hot quiche
   tastes of disappointingly little.

CHAPTER 2

Meat and Fish

*I*f an egg is the perfect plaything for the creative cook, meat deserves to be taken more seriously. After all, those creatures didn't die to be cremated and served on a bed of boil-in-the-bag rice by someone eager to get back to the Friday film. They deserve better. Always buy the best meat you can afford — not only because it's likely to have been treated better, but because the end result will almost certainly make you happier. Look at labels, and if you have a local farmers' market, or butcher or fishmonger, use them, if only in conjunction with the supermarket — they're likely to be able to give you advice on cheaper cuts, and how to cook them, and they're a good source of things like bones for stock, and less popular, but more sustainable species of fish. Eat less, but better — *Julie & Julia* author Julie Powell says that the six months she spent as a butcher's apprentice for her second book, *Cleaving*, made her eat less meat, rather than more ('I only want to eat the stuff where I know where it comes from,' she told the *Huffington Post*). Try out new cuts and recipes (tasty chicken thigh instead of bland breast, shin of beef stew rather than frying steak) and your cookery will benefit no end.

In this country, we're still scared of cooking fish – but the most basic recipes are so simple they're hardly worth including here. Just about any fresh fish fillet will be delicious if you put it in a lightly greased, loosely-wrapped foil parcel along with a splash of white wine, a slice of lemon and some herbs, or some grated fresh ginger, chilli and soy sauce, pop it in an 180°C oven and bake for 15 minutes – you can tell it's cooked when the flesh is opaque, and flakes easily. If it isn't done, simply put it back for a couple of minutes and then try again. This also works with whole fish, but depending on their size, they'll take a little longer – which is why it pays to invest in a fish cookery book.

I rely heavily on the two River Cottage and Leiths Cookery School books on the subject of meat and fish – Hugh is helpful for getting you fired up about great meat and fish, as well as for more unusual recipe ideas, and Leiths is invaluable on technique. And, if you're more grown up than me, Fergus Henderson of St John is very good on offal – I'm cooking my way through *Nose to Tail Eating* in the hope that one day I'll come round to the idea.

Perfect
Roast Chicken

Jean Anthelme Brillat-Savarin, the nineteenth-century French gourmet — and inspiration for the unfeasibly rich triple-cream cheese of the same name — described the humble chicken as a culinary blank canvas, and he's got a point. Viewed with the appropriate respect, even the simplest of chicken dishes, the roast, is revealed as a veritable Tardis of gastronomic potential — it might sound like an easy option, but actually it's a surprisingly difficult thing to get right, which is why it's often used by chefs as a test for potential new recruits. The issue is not so much one of flavour — you get what you pay for in that department — but of texture: how do you achieve a delectably crisp skin while keeping the meat nice and juicy?

Brining, stuffing, slow-roasting at 60°C, all have their advocates online, but lazily, I'm drawn to the Californian Thomas Keller's suitably laid-back recipe, which sounds perfect for a Sunday afternoon. No basting, no buttering — just a smoking hot oven and a little seasoning. It's easy, and the skin is tear-jerkingly crisp, but sadly, at the expense of the meat, which is rather dry.

Pierre Koffman, whose Chelsea restaurant La Tante Claire was one of the first British kitchens to win three Michelin stars, has a more hands-on approach — but although turning the bird at regular intervals and basting it with goose fat makes the flesh undeniably succulent, there's no excusing its pallid, greasy skin. Slow-roasting it until the temperature reaches a bacteria-zonking 62°C, as the *Guardian* food writer Matthew Fort suggests, proves far too much hassle – I'm up until 1 a.m., and the thing still isn't cooked through.

Former Bibendum chef Simon Hopkinson's traditional approach, given in his much-fêted first cookbook, *Roast Chicken and Other Stories*, involves smearing the skin with butter and treating the bird to an initial blast in a hot oven, before turning the temperature down to a more reasonable 190°C. It's a successful enough result, but I'm finally won over by *Mail on Sunday* cookery writer Annie Bell's nifty poach and roast combo. The meat is deliciously tender, and, after turning the dial right up to finish the chicken off, I've got a crisp skin too. Truly, the world holds no more beautiful sight.

> **1 medium free-range chicken,**
>   **about 1.6kg (removed from the**
>   **fridge an hour before cooking)**
> **1 head of garlic, cut in half laterally**
> **4 sprigs of thyme, leaves only**
> **1 tablespoon olive oil**
> **Salt and pepper**
> **1 lemon, cut in half**

1. Preheat the oven to 220°C/425°F/gas 7. Bring a large pan of salted water to the boil, remove any trussing string from the chicken and add it to the pan, breast side down. Turn down the heat and simmer for 10 minutes. Remove from the water and pat thoroughly dry: you can use a hairdryer to help if you have one handy.

2. Put the garlic into a roasting tin and scatter half the thyme over the top. Put the chicken on top of it and rub with the oil. Season generously, both inside and out, scatter with the rest of the thyme and put the lemon inside the cavity. Tip a couple of millimetres of just-boiled water from the kettle or hot stock into the bottom of the tin, and put into the oven for 1 hour and 15 minutes, or until the juices run clear: insert a skewer or the top of a knife into the thickest part of the thigh and then press down to check this.

3. Ten minutes before the end of cooking, tip out the juices to save for gravy if you're making one (see page 166), and turn up the oven temperature as high as it will go to help crisp the skin. Keep an eye on it to prevent it burning.

4. Allow the chicken to rest in a warm place for 15 minutes before carving and serving with the roasted garlic.

Perfect
Chicken Pie

*P*ies are God's gift to the cook — a medley of ingredients, prettily gift-wrapped in pastry, which will have your dinner guests falling over themselves in greed and gratitude. Just about any foodstuff is improved by a crisp, golden crust, but I think chicken works particularly well; the creamy white sauce keeps it moist, and is the perfect showcase for its delicate flavour. You can, of course, make this pie with leftover roast chicken, as Nigella does, but poaching a bird for it is well worth the effort; it gives a juicier result, and there's something for everyone inside. Buying a good-quality whole bird will also work out cheaper than buying enough chicken pieces for everyone.

Like Nigella, *delicious* magazine food editor Angela Boggiano tops the chicken and tarragon pie in her recipe collection, *Pie*, with rich shortcrust, but I find I prefer a rough puff, as used by Jamie Oliver — crisp and flaky on top, delectably soggy beneath. Angela's chicken comes in a cream and white wine sauce which is a little bit thin for my taste, although I'm sold on the leeks and tarragon she uses to flavour it: both underused flavours that work brilliantly with chicken.

Skye Gyngell uses crème fraîche in her pie instead, but I don't like the slightly sour note this gives: sometimes the simplest ideas, like Nigella's white sauce, are the best. Here I've flavoured it with the poaching liquid (if you're using cooked chicken you can, like her, substitute chicken stock) and enriched it with a little cream so it wraps around the meat like a comfort blanket. Serve with steamed greens.

Serves 6

1 small chicken, about 1.4kg
1 large carrot, quartered
1 large onion, quartered
2 sticks of celery, quartered
A few parsley stalks
1 bay leaf
A few black peppercorns
40g butter, plus a knob for cooking
2 leeks, thinly sliced
4 rashers of streaky bacon, chopped
2 tablespoons plain flour
250ml milk
4 tablespoons single cream
A small bunch of tarragon, leaves chopped
Salt and pepper
1 quantity of rough puff pastry (see page 187)
1 free-range egg, beaten

1. Put the chicken into a pan large enough to hold it comfortably and add the carrot, onion, celery, parsley, bay leaf and peppercorns. Cover with cold water and bring to the boil, then lower the heat and poach for about an hour, until cooked through, skimming any scum from the top every now and then.
2. Remove the chicken to a plate, draining the juices from the cavity as you go. Strain the poaching liquid, put it back into

the pan on a strong heat and reduce the liquid by half, which should take about half an hour. Meanwhile, pull the meat off the chicken in large chunks (you can keep the carcass for stock – it will be fine in the freezer for a couple of months).

3. Preheat the oven to 180°C/350°F/gas 4. Put a knob of butter into a frying pan and gently sweat the leeks until softened; add the bacon and cook for 5 minutes, then turn off the heat. Melt the rest of the butter in a medium saucepan over a low heat, and stir in the flour. Cook, stirring, for a couple of minutes, without allowing it to brown (cooking the flour is vital; raw flour will spoil the taste of the sauce), then gradually whisk in about 150ml of the reduced poaching liquid, and then the milk and cream – if you add it too fast, your sauce will be lumpy. Beat until smooth, then simmer gently for about 10 minutes, until thickened. Stir through the tarragon and season to taste. (You can freeze the rest of the poaching liquid to use as a stock.)

4. Stir the chicken, leeks and bacon into the sauce, and spoon into a pie dish. Roll the rough puff out on a floured surface until about 5mm thick. Brush the edges of the pie dish with beaten egg, then lay the pastry over the pie and press down around the edges with a fork to seal it. Cut a small hole in the centre to let the steam out, and brush with beaten egg. Put into the oven and cook for about 45 minutes, until the pastry is well risen and golden.

Other great pies
Braising steak and ale; ham and leek; Cheshire cheese and onion; mince and potato; venison and red wine; lamb and thyme; spinach and feta; Stargazy (or Cornish fish pie)

Perfect
Coq au Vin

*T*his is a dish that, in my mind, will be forever associated with the late, great Keith Floyd — it's the kind of cunningly rustic French cookery he delighted in, designed to wring every last ounce of flavour from bargain-basement ingredients. It's not going to win any prizes for thrift these days, elderly cockerels and rough local wines being hard to come by for most of us, but be reassured, this brief trip down memory lane is worth every centime.

Simon Hopkinson and Lindsey Bareham note in the preface to their recipe that 'it would have to be a complete moron who managed to cock up a coq au vin', but I fear this may have been more for the sheer pleasure of the wordplay; it may be hard to make chicken, red wine, bacon and shallots taste bad, but equally, the dish requires thought.

First of all: you must use chicken legs and thighs; poaching a whole bird, as Anthony Bourdain does in his *Les Halles Cookbook*, is not only cumbersome, but leaves one with a chicken with sauce, rather than a coherent stew. Using bone-in pieces will help to make the dish rich and unctuous — and the hard-working meat stands up better to slow cooking than leaner, more delicately flavoured breasts. Bourdain marinates his chicken in wine and aromatics overnight before cooking, but I prefer to take Simon and Lindsey's advice and cook my coq au vin a day in advance, to give the flavours time to meld.

Elizabeth David uses a mixture of chicken stock and wine in *French Provincial Cooking*, and prepares the sauce first, as, she says, in traditional recipes it is 'difficult to get the sauce to the right consistency without spoiling the bird by overcooking'. The principle is sound, and much easier than Richard Olney's method in *The French Menu Cookbook*, which has one whipping chicken pieces in and out of the sauce as if tongs were going out of fashion. His wine and cognac sauce is pleasingly robustly flavoured, though, while David's dish ends up rather dry.

As its name suggests, wine is an important part of this recipe, so don't just pop down to the corner for a plastic bottle of cooking stuff – although it doesn't have to be from Burgundy, you'll get the best results from a silky, fruity Pinot Noir. If you find the finished sauce is too thin and acidic, a spoonful of redcurrant jelly, as used by Hopkinson and Bareham, should save the day – but it's easier to buy the right wine in the first place.

Olney finishes his 'chicken in red wine' off in the oven, which I think is a waste of energy for no discernible gain, but I like the idea, common to many recipes, of introducing the vegetables towards the end of cooking; they become pappy if you put them in at the beginning, as in the recipe in *The Prawn Cocktail Years*. Both Larousse and Julia Child recommend thickening the sauce with flour to finish it off, but flouring the chicken before cooking should be sufficient to bind everything together – this is not a hearty stew in the British or Irish sense of the word, but something a little more refined, after all. Serve with boiled potatoes or plain rice, a green salad, and a toast to Keith.

Serves 4

I bottle of Pinot Noir
I carrot, roughly chopped
I stick of celery, roughly chopped
I small onion, cut into quarters
5 cloves of garlic, 4 of them peeled
   and lightly crushed with the flat
   edge of a knife, the other one
   peeled and finely sliced
I bay leaf
A small bunch of thyme
I tablespoon butter
150g piece of smoked streaky bacon,
   cut into thick chunks
2 tablespoons plain flour
Salt and pepper
4 chicken thighs
2 chicken legs
20 baby onions or 10 shallots, peeled
   but left whole (drop them briefly into
   boiling water first, to loosen the skins)
20 button mushrooms, or 10 white
   mushrooms, quartered
4 tablespoons Cognac

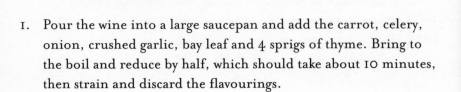

1. Pour the wine into a large saucepan and add the carrot, celery,
    onion, crushed garlic, bay leaf and 4 sprigs of thyme. Bring to
    the boil and reduce by half, which should take about 10 minutes,
    then strain and discard the flavourings.

2. Heat the butter over a medium-high flame in a large, heavy-based pan with a lid and add the bacon. Cook until golden, then lift out with a slotted spoon and put aside. Meanwhile, tip the flour on to a plate and season well. Roll the chicken pieces in it to coat them.

3. Put the chicken into the pan, in batches if necessary, brown well on all sides, then lift out and put with the bacon. (Your bacon should have given off enough fat for there still to be enough in the pan for the next stage, but if not, add another tablespoon of butter or a glug of oil.)

4. Turn the heat down to medium-low and add the onions or shallots. Cook for about 10 minutes, turning occasionally, until they are beginning to caramelize, then add the mushrooms and the sliced garlic, cook for a further 4 minutes, then lift out of the pan and set aside (but not with the meat).

5. Turn up the heat, pour a little of the reduced wine into the pan and scrape the bits off the bottom with a wooden spoon, then put in the chicken and the bacon, keeping a few bits of the latter back as garnish. Pour over the brandy and set it alight, and then, when the flames have gone out, add the rest of the wine and thyme leaves. Bring to the boil, turn down the heat, cover and simmer gently for an hour.

6. Add the onions, mushrooms and garlic and simmer for another 20 minutes, keeping the lid only half on this time. Taste for seasoning and serve with the rest of the bacon sprinkled over the top, and some boiled potatoes or rice – if you're making it the day before you want to eat, which will improve its flavour, lift the solidified fat off the top before reheating.

Perfect
Irish Stew

*I*rish stew, as a friend of mine observed bitterly after being let down by her family recipe at a dinner party, represents the less glamorous end of *cucina povera*; the watery, potato-heavy aspect of kitchen thrift that no one likes to mention. No stock or herbs here to give the dish a boost – why, for some purists, even a carrot is unnecessarily exotic.

Fortunately, it's a dish that can be updated without desecration – Dublin-born chef Richard Corrigan, for example, replaces the traditional water with homemade lamb stock. Most butchers will give you bones for free if you ask nicely, so it's even in keeping with the thrifty spirit of the original, and it gives an infinitely better flavour. He uses filleted middle neck – neck is a great cut for slow cooking, but leaving the bones in, as in the Ballymaloe recipe (which, extravagantly, uses chops instead), helps to give the gravy body. Not everyone likes picking meat off the bone, of course, so I've used a mixture – let the fussy fish around for their supper.

Although I scoffed at Corrigan's request for two sorts of potato, after cooking his stew I was forced to admit it's a brilliant idea; the floury bits break down to thicken the sauce, and the waxy ones stay nice and firm – I simmer mine on top, as in the Ballymaloe stew, so they steam as the meat cooks. I've also added turnips, because I like them, but just stick another carrot in instead if you don't.

You can cook this in a low oven, but it's more traditional to let it bubble gently away on the stove for a couple of hours, until the meat falls off the bone. Draining the fat from the gravy is another tip I picked up from the Cork cookery school; you could also whisk in a tablespoon of melted butter and flour at this point to thicken it, but then you really would be flying in the face of convention.

If you can find mutton, give it a try here — it's the perfect vehicle for its slightly stronger flavour, and slow cooking will render it meltingly tender. Serve with steamed greens and chunks of soda bread to mop up all those lovely juices.

Serves 6

1kg lamb or mutton bones
5 carrots
1 onion, halved
½ a stick of celery, roughly chopped
1 bay leaf
5 peppercorns, bruised by lightly
    crushing with the flat side of a knife
A small bunch of thyme
Salt and pepper
2 small turnips
12 baby onions (often sold as pickling
    onions) or shallots, or 6 small onions
1 large floury potato (e.g. Maris Piper,
    King Edward) and 12 small waxy
    potatoes (e.g. Desiree)

**800g middle neck of lamb or mutton,
   bone in and roughly chopped
500g deboned stewing lamb
25g butter**

1. Put the bones into a large pan with 1 roughly chopped carrot,
    the halved onion, celery, bay leaf, peppercorns and a large sprig
    of thyme. Cover with 3 litres of cold water, bring to the boil,
    skimming off the scum from the top, then simmer, uncovered,
    for 2 hours. Pour through a fine sieve and discard the bones and
    vegetables, then return the liquid to the pan and simmer until
    reduced to about 1 litre of stock. Season.
2. Chop the remaining carrots and the turnips into large chunks,
    peel the onions and, if larger than baby onions, cut them into
    quarters. Peel the potatoes, and cut the floury one into large cubes.
3. Cut any chunks of fat off the meat, and put into a large pan on a
    high heat, along with the butter. Brown the meat on all sides, in
    batches, then put it into a casserole dish. Cook the onions in the
    fat for 5 minutes, stirring, then add to the meat. Do the same
    with the carrots, the turnip and the floury potato.
4. Deglaze the pan with the lamb stock, scraping to get all the crusty
    bits off the bottom, and pour this over the meat and vegetables.
    Season, and add a few sprigs of thyme. Arrange the waxy potatoes
    on top and bring to the boil, then turn the heat down and
    simmer gently for 2 hours, covered, until the lamb is tender.
5. Tip the meat and vegetables into a colander set above a large
    bowl. Pass the broth through a gravy separator to remove most
    of the fat, or, alternatively, allow it to sit through a few minutes,
    and then spoon off as much of the fat as rises to the top as you
    can. Pour back over the meat and allow to sit for 15 minutes
    before serving.

Good cuts of meat for slow cooking

Cheaper cuts of meat generally come from older animals, or hard-working bits of younger animals — they will have a high proportion of tough connective tissue, which must be broken down by long, slow simmering. This also breaks down the muscle fibres, and results in meat that's often so meltingly tender and unctuous that it can be cut with a spoon. Getting the best out of these cuts takes time — although not necessarily much of yours; they're quite happy to simmer away quietly for hours on a low heat while you read the paper, or watch a film — but I think the results are infinitely more delicious than the most tender fillet steak.

Beef: blade, brisket, chuck, flank, leg, middle ribs, neck, oxtail, shin, silverside, skirt
Lamb: breast, chump, leg, neck and middle neck, scrag end, shank, shoulder
Pork: belly, chump end, hand, leg, loin, spare rib
Chicken: thighs and legs

Perfect
Burgers

*T*he hamburger may well have European origins — it's thought to
have crossed the Atlantic with the German immigrants of the early
nineteenth century — but it took the Americans to recognize what
North Carolina-born author Tom Robbins once termed this
'companionable and faintly erotic' chunk of seasoned beef as
comfort food extraordinaire. Even if you tuck into seven colours of
caviar every weekend, I bet the scent of grilling burgers still gets you
all Pavlov's dog around the chops. It's that primal, charred, slightly
crunchy exterior, the soft juiciness within — and of course, that
perfect combination of toppings, chosen in childhood and sacred
thereafter.

There's no place for lean, or finely ground beef in a
burger — both produce a dry, crumbly patty unworthy
of the name. Heston Blumenthal recommends a
2:1:1 combination of chuck, short rib and brisket,
but in my experience, plain old chuck will do nicely.
Ideally, of course, you would mince your beef yourself,
but if you have neither the time, nor the appropriate food processor
attachment, ask your butcher to do it for you — a coarse mince gives
the best texture.

Homemade burgers can be disappointingly dense; throwing in a few
breadcrumbs is a surefire way of lightening the texture. They will
also soak up whatever liquid you use to bind the burger together,

keeping it nice and juicy: egg, as recommended by *Larousse Gastronomique*, gives an oddly crunchy result once cooked, and the dollop of cream used by larger-than-life *Evening Standard* food writer Charles Campion in his excellent barbecue book, *Food from Fire*, makes them unnecessarily rich — you couldn't top these babies with cheese.

Campion's Guinness burgers are inspired, however — the stout makes the burgers tender, juicy and super beefy, while caramelized onion adds a touch of sweetness. Poking a dimple in the middle of the patties before cooking is a handy tip I gleaned from *Leiths Meat Bible* — it stops them turning into cannonballs on the grill. Chilling them before cooking will help keep them together when you cook them: whatever you do, don't press them down in the manner of a Hollywood diner cook, however — you'll lose all those delicious juices.

I must add that, in the interests of food safety, the Department of Health advises we should cook all minced meat products right through, until the juices run clear and there is no pink meat left. This is obviously particularly important for young children, pregnant women and the elderly, or anyone else with what is known as a 'compromised immune system'. The rest of you should weigh up risk versus reward, and make your own decision on the matter — but if you come down in favour of reducing quality beef to a dry puck of overcooked protein, you're not coming to my barbecue.

Serves 6

1 tablespoon olive oil or soft butter,
   plus extra to brush
1 large onion, finely chopped
1kg coarse-ground beef mince
100ml stout
2 tablespoons brown breadcrumbs
2 teaspoons finely chopped herbs
   (parsley or thyme work well)
1 teaspoon salt
Black pepper
Garnishes as desired (6 small sesame or wholemeal
   rolls, 6 x 20g slices of mature Cheddar, sliced
   pickles, sliced tomato, iceberg lettuce leaves,
   mustard, ketchup, tomato relish – the choice
   is yours)

1. Heat the oil or butter in a frying pan over a low heat, and cook
   the onion for 20 minutes, until soft and slightly browned. Leave
   to cool.
2. Spread the beef out on a tray and sprinkle over the onion. Add
   the stout, breadcrumbs, herbs and seasoning and mix together
   with a fork, being careful not to overwork it.
3. Divide the meat into twelve flattish burgers, putting a dimple in the
   centre of each to help keep them flat during cooking. Cover and
   refrigerate for an hour. Lightly brush with melted butter or oil.
4. Cook the burgers on a medium to hot barbecue or griddle pan:
   leave them undisturbed for the first 3 minutes so they build
   up a good seal on the bottom, then carefully turn them over,
   adding a slice of cheese on top if using. Cook for a further

4 minutes for rare, and 7 for well done, and allow to rest for a few minutes before serving. (You can toast buns, cut-side down, on the barbecue at this point.) Put the garnishes and sauces on the table, so people can build their own perfect burgers.

Barbecue tips

Take the barbecue seriously. If you've put the effort into buying the food, there's no point in wandering off to watch the football while it burns. Barbecues are notoriously unreliable, so keep an eye on it, even if you're reading the paper or following a conversation with the other one.

Oil the grill itself, but only once the barbecue is hot enough to actually cook on – it will just be burnt off if you put it on too early.

Don't add any food until the flames die down to reveal grey embers.

Although barbecues and ovens are very different beasts, it's helpful to think of the heat it's giving off in the same terms. In *12,167 Kitchen and Cooking Secrets*, Susan Sampson reveals a no-pain-no-gain approach to judging the temperature of a grill. If you can hold your hand just above the grill for less than a second before it's too hot for comfort, then it's very hot (260°C or more); 1–2 seconds and it's hot (between 200 and 260°C); 3–4 seconds and it's medium (180–200°C); 5 seconds and it's medium-low (160–180°C) and 6 or more seconds means the temperature is low (150°C or less).

Perfect
Sausages

*L*ike beer and biscuits, the great British banger is something we, as a nation, can be proud of. Not for us the suspiciously smooth German *Wurst*, or the startlingly sweet Chinese *lap cheung*: our plump beauties pair serious texture with subtle seasoning – a sun-dried tomato, for example, has no place in a hog casing this far from the Mediterranean. Yet somewhat perplexingly, we're also a people who sincerely believe that stabbing a sausage and shoving it under a hot grill is doing it justice.

 My mother always presaged death, or at the very least, painful blinding by molten pig fat, for anyone who didn't prick their links before cooking. As every good foodie knows, this is nonsense: rationing ended some time ago, and these days even the cheapest banger is unlikely to contain enough water to actually explode. *Guardian* food writer Matthew Fort claims it makes sausages dry and flavourless, and he's right – and subsequent grilling is even worse. A good sausage deserves slow cooking in a pan with a little butter – the glossy plump results are well worth forty-five minutes wait. Don't bother poaching them first, as Heston Blumenthal does – it's a lot of effort for a grey banger, and a pile of extra washing up. Serve with fluffy mash (see page 102), a big pile of peas and a pot of English mustard.

A knob of butter
Sausages

1. Heat a knob of butter in a generously sized, heavy-based frying pan over a low heat. You may need two, depending on how many sausages you're cooking; the important thing is not to overcrowd them, or they'll poach in their own juices rather than frying.
2. When the butter has melted, put in the sausages and fry very gently for about 45 minutes, turning once or twice during that time. They should leave a sticky, caramelized residue on the bottom of the pan – which should be scoffed by the cook before serving.

Perfect
Cottage Pie

*T*his is neither the time nor the place to get into an argument about the semantics of shepherd's versus cottage pie. I think we can all agree that it makes sense, logically speaking, for the first to refer to a dish made with lamb, and that by long custom, the second has come to suggest beef, whatever the original relationship between the two.

The truth is, although you may choose to vary the herbs, the two meats are largely interchangeable in this context, as most recipes acknowledge. Once lubricated by a rich, savoury gravy and entombed beneath a blanket of crisp-topped mash, few hungry souls would notice the difference in any case.

What is important is to have juicy, robustly textured meat — although Hugh Fearnley-Whittingstall's leftover roast beef and Nigel Slater's mince both work fine here, it's Jane Grigson's finely chopped chuck which proves the perfect partner for the fluffy potato topping. It has a more robust feel to it, rather than simply melting into the sauce. (I think you do need to peel the spuds, here, by the way, to enjoy the contrast in textures.)

Forget her garlic and white wine though — this homely dish needs no such Mediterranean makeover, nor does it require Simon

Hopkinson and Lindsey Bareham's tomato ketchup, which I can taste even after forty minutes in the oven. Nigel's simple sauce of stock, Worcestershire sauce and thyme is perfect, the condiment giving the meat depth and a hint of spice without overpowering it — I've just added a touch of cornflour to make a more satisfying gravy. Any further additions are at your own risk.

Serves 4

> **1kg floury potatoes, such as**
>   **Maris Piper, peeled**
> **Salt and pepper**
> **600g shin of beef (trimmed weight),**
>   **chopped into small pieces**
> **25g beef dripping or butter**
> **2 onions, finely diced**
> **2 carrots, finely diced**
> **2 sticks of celery, finely diced**
> **1 teaspoon dried thyme**
> **350ml good-quality beef stock**
> **1 teaspoon cornflour**
> **1 teaspoon Worcestershire sauce**
> **125g butter**

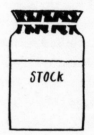

1. Cut your potatoes into evenly-sized chunks and put into a large pan of cold, salted water. Bring to the boil and simmer until tender.
2. Cut the trimmed beef into evenly-sized dice, then gather these together on a chopping board. Grasp the handles of two knives together in one hand, and using your other hand to keep the two

tips in place, move the knives back and forth across the meat to chop it into Icm pieces.

3. Meanwhile, heat the dripping, if you have any left over from your last roast, or 25g butter in a pan over a moderate heat, then add the vegetables and cover. Cook for 20 minutes, until soft but not brown.

4. Add the thyme, then turn up the heat and add the beef. Cook for 5 minutes, stirring to brown all over, then add half the stock. Whisk the other half with the cornflour, and stir into the meat mixture. Add a generous dash of Worcestershire sauce, turn down the heat, and allow to simmer uncovered for I hour and 15 minutes, until the meat is tender.

5. Drain the potatoes and mash with I00g of the butter. Season to taste.

6. Taste and season the meat, adding more Worcestershire sauce if necessary. If it looks dry, pour in a little water.

7. Preheat the oven to I80°C/350°F/gas 4. Put the meat into a large baking dish (30 x 28cm would be ideal) and allow to cool slightly if you've got time — it will make adding the potato easier. For a nice crispy top, I like to spoon it on in lumps: you can run a fork over the top if you prefer. Dot with the remaining 25g of butter.

8. Put into the oven and bake for 40–50 minutes, until the potato is crisp and slightly brown, then serve.

How to keep cut herbs fresh
Treat them like a bunch of flowers: cut a few millimetres off the bottom of the stem, then put them into a couple of centimetres of water in

the fridge, making sure no leaves are submerged. Change the water every day.

Alternatively, you can wrap the bottom of the herbs in a damp piece of kitchen roll and put them in an open plastic bag in the salad tray of the fridge.

Perfect
Steak

Some myths can be as irritatingly persistent as a dog at a barbecue. Most of us, I think, can accept that you don't get piles from sitting on radiators, and that the world didn't hatch from an eagle's egg — yet still we cling to the idea that searing meat magically 'locks in' the juices, and no wonder, with the likes of Delia and Gordon waffling on about sealing things.

In fact, every time you hear a chef on TV mention the word 'seal', you should fire off a meatily worded letter of complaint, because this idea, which has been hanging around since Aristotle was a lad, has been acknowledged as bunkum for about eighty years. The clue is in the lovely sizzling noise that meat makes when it hits a hot surface like a pan — that's the sound of water evaporating. You will notice that it doesn't stop when, after a minute or so, you decide that side of the joint is sealed. That's because it isn't; moisture is still leaking out through that gorgeously charred surface, and will continue to do so for some minutes after you finish the 'sealing' process.

However, after experimenting with a variety of cooking heats and times, from slower cooking as favoured by Alain Ducasse, who collects Michelin stars like most chefs collect blue plasters (which works well for very thick pieces of meat, less so for more normal-sized steaks), to finishing them off in the oven à la John Torode, I realized that Hugh Fearnley-Whittingstall was, as usual, right: although briefly searing steak on a high temperature doesn't make it perceptibly juicier — if anything, it was slightly drier — it does improve the flavour, thanks to the workings of the Maillard reaction in that wonderfully savoury, carbonized crust. (The Maillard reaction is another name for the browning of sugars and amino acids which is responsible for much of the flavour of roasted and grilled foods.) Even advocates of very slow cooking, like Heston and his eighteen-hour fore rib, finish steaks off with a quick blast in a hot pan.

Buy the best-quality steak you can afford — depending on the cut, it should have a good marbling of creamy fat, and be slightly dark, rather than bright red, indicating that it's been aged to tenderize the meat and improve the flavour. For cooking at home, I like rump — it has bags of flavour and is easy to get right. Look for one that's about 4cm thick — any thinner and you'll risk overcooking it.

> **Steak of your choice — allow about
>   300g per person, depending
>   on appetite
> A knob of butter
> Salt and pepper**

1. Bring the steaks to room temperature before cooking, and put plates in a low oven to heat. Put a heavy-based frying pan on a high heat, and grease it with a little butter — a good piece of rump or sirloin will give off its own fat, and too much liquid will interfere with your flavourful crust. Cut off a small piece of

meat to use as a test — it should sizzle when it hits the pan, but the pan shouldn't be smoking.

2. Add the steaks to the pan — don't overcrowd them, and cook in batches if necessary. Leave them for a minute, then turn them over. If the pan's at the right temperature, they should be nicely browned, but not black. Season, and cook for another minute before repeating the process: although exact cooking times will depend on the size of your steak, Hugh Fearnley-Whittingstall's suggestion of 3–4 minutes for rare, 5–6 for medium rare, 6–8 for medium, and 10 for well done always works for me. The old rule of thumb (page 57) is a good one.

3. Remove the steaks from the pan and put on to warm plates for 5 minutes to rest before serving. When you've finished, you can deglaze the pan with a little red wine and pour the juices over the steaks.

Marinade

Marinating a good steak is a crying shame, but it's a useful tool to have in reserve for tougher cuts, such as onglet (also known as thick skirt in this country), and also works well with lamb leg or shoulder steaks, or chicken thighs — particularly on the barbecue. This recipe, based on the flavours of an Argentinean *chimichurri*, but harnessing the tenderizing properties of yoghurt instead of vinegar, which I found made the meat tough, is a great one to keep in mind for barbecue season.

Makes enough for 6 steaks or chicken breasts

200g Greek yoghurt
A large bunch (about 40g) of
    fresh herbs of your choice, finely
    chopped (parsley, mint and
    coriander work particularly well)
2 teaspoons salt
4 cloves of garlic, crushed
6 spring onions, finely chopped
1 small green chilli, finely chopped

Mix all the ingredients together, then use to coat each piece of meat well. Put the meat into a freezer bag or a shallow bowl and refrigerate for at least 3 hours, or overnight. Bring to room temperature before cooking.

Rule of thumb

Although it's not an exact science, this is a useful way to judge how your steaks are cooked without cutting into them, as well as being a slightly gruesome reminder that we're all made of meat. Prod the thickest part of the steak with a clean finger, and then compare it to your own hand.

Rare: will feel like the pad of flesh at the bottom of
    your thumb when your hand is completely relaxed
    – soft but springy.
Medium rare: will feel like that same pad of flesh

when you touch the tip of your index finger to the tip of the thumb on the same hand.

Medium: will feel like that flesh when you touch the tip of your middle finger to the tip of the thumb (are you getting the idea?).

Medium well done: will feel like that flesh when you touch the tip of your ring finger to the tip of the same thumb.

Well done: will feel like that flesh when you touch the tip of your little finger to the tip of the same thumb.

Perfect
Ragù Bolognese

*T*o write on spag bol is to wade into a mire of controversy thicker
and darker than any ragù that ever came out of nonna's kitchen.
People feel very strongly indeed about what is, basically, a meat sauce
of no more particular merit than, say, a shepherd's pie, or a chilli
— and almost every cookery book has its own 'authentic' version.

I'm all for keeping things simple, but the minimalist
beef, vegetable and tomato purée version in the
classic Italian recipe bible *The Silver Spoon* fails
to deliver on flavour, and although a dollop
of cream can generally be relied upon to
improve any dish, Italian cookery teacher Ursula
Ferrigno's unctuous bolognese is rich but bland. I like the dark and
intensely savoury ragù in Locatelli's *Made in Italy*, but the mixture of
red wine and tomato passata doesn't seem to be typical of the
traditional sauces of the area, unlike Marcella Hazan's combination
of milk and white wine. The Italian–American food writer claims the
dairy counteracts the acidic 'bite' of the alcohol — and it certainly
adds a hint of sweetness to the end result. Bologna, in the north-
east of Italy, is cow country, so this addition makes sense.

Although mixing meats is quite usual in the dish's homeland, I find
adding pork overpowers the beef: chicken livers and pancetta,
however, as used by Elizabeth David, add a subtle smokiness to the
sauce. (She takes her recipe from one Zia Nerina, 'a splendid

woman, titanic of proportion but angelic of face and manner', who ran a renowned restaurant in Bologna in the 1950s, when David was researching *Italian Food*.) Lastly, cooking the dish very slowly and gently in the oven, in obedience to Heston Blumenthal, makes the meat meltingly tender, and wonderfully rich. It may seem a lot of faff for such a common or garden dish, so remember, this is *ragù alla bolognese*, not spag bol — and you certainly won't regret it.

The fact is that there is no definitive recipe for a bolognese meat sauce, but to be worthy of the name, it should respect the traditions of the area: white wine, meat and milk, rather than tomatoes or Chianti, should be the key flavours. Cook long and slow, freeze any extra for week-night suppers, and serve with anything but spaghetti; in Bologna, rich meat ragùs such as this are eaten with fresh tagliatelle, or spinach-tinted lasagne verdi. Tag bol doesn't have quite the same ring to it though, does it?

Serves 4

A generous knob of butter
100g dry cure smoked streaky
   bacon, finely diced
1 onion, finely diced
1 carrot, finely diced
2 sticks of celery, finely diced
250g coarsely minced beef, at
   room temperature
Salt and pepper
40g chicken livers, finely chopped
150ml whole milk

Nutmeg, to grate
150ml dry white wine
1 x 400g tin of plum tomatoes
500g homemade pasta (see page 89)
    or dried pasta of your choice
100g Parmesan or pecorino, to serve

1. Melt the butter in a large flameproof casserole set over a gentle
    heat, then add the bacon. Cook for 5 minutes, until the bacon
    has started to melt, then add the onion and cook gently for a
    further 5 minutes, until softened. Tip in the carrot and cook for
    5 minutes before adding the celery and cooking for a further
    2 minutes.
2. Turn the heat up, crumble the beef into the pan, season
    generously and brown for 5 minutes, stirring occasionally to
    break up any lumps. Stir in the liver, and let it cook for another
    5 minutes.
3. Preheat the oven to 125°C/250°F/gas ½. Pour in the milk,
    and grate a little nutmeg over the top. Turn the heat down and
    simmer gently for 30 minutes, until almost all the milk has
    evaporated.
4. Pour in the wine and the tomatoes, breaking them up with the
    back of a wooden spoon, and stir well. Bring to a simmer. Put
    the casserole into the oven, with the lid slightly askew, and cook
    for at least 3 hours (4 is even better), until the meat is very
    tender. Check on it occasionally, and top up with a little water if
    it seems too dry, although this probably won't be necessary.
5. Cook the pasta in a large pan of generously salted water and
    drain. Add the sauce to the pasta and toss together well to coat
    before serving with freshly grated Parmesan or pecorino.

Pasta, meet sauce

Although you're free to eat vermicelli with wild
boar ragù, or strozzapreti with pesto if you so wish
– hell, you can top it with custard and call it Sheila
if that's what floats your boat – certain shapes just
go better with particular sauces. The general rule is,
the more delicate the pasta, the more delicate the
sauce – angel hair (capellini) goes well with a simple
oil and garlic dressing, for example, while chunky
rigatoni can stand up to baking with minced beef.
Here's a brief guide to matching some of the more
widely available shapes with recipes – you'll notice
the most versatile shapes are the thicker noodles, like
fettuccine, and smaller shapes, like farfalle (bows),
which go with just about everything.

Baked: bucatini, fusilli, lasagne, macaroni, orzo,
   penne, radiatori, rigatoni, rotini
Butter or oil-based sauces: capellini, farfalle,
   fettuccine, fusilli, linguine, macaroni, penne,
   spaghetti, tagliatelle

Cream or cheese-based sauces: capellini,
   farfalle, fettuccine, fusilli, lasagne, linguine,
   macaroni, penne, rigatoni, rotini, spaghetti,
   tagliatelle
Meat: conchiglie, farfalle, fettuccine, fusilli,
   lasagne, linguine, macaroni, orecchiette,
   pappardelle, rigatoni, spaghetti alla chitarra,
   tagliatelle

Pesto: capellini, farfalle, fusilli, linguine,
   trofie

Seafood: capellini, farfalle, fettuccine, linguine, spaghetti, spaghetti alla chitarra, tagliatelle

Tomato: bucatini, capellini, conchiglie, farfalle, fettuccine, fusilli, lasagne, linguine, macaroni, orecchiette, penne, radiatori, rigatoni, rotini, spaghetti, spaghetti alla chitarra, tagliatelle

Perfect
Roast Pork with Crackling

I'm happy to confess to being an out-and-proud fat-fancier. The tender, melting wobble of it, that satisfying oily crunch – how can mere meat hope to compete? Good as it tastes, fat is largely a textural pleasure, and crackling is surely the supreme example of this: a blistered top, as dry and crunchy as an autumn leaf, hiding a layer of unctuous, creamy deliciousness beneath.

The basic principles of great crackling are simple enough. You must score the rind in vertical lines about a finger's width apart, to allow the heat to penetrate the fat, but without cutting into the meat itself – go down too far, and all the lovely juices will come rushing out, which is definitely not desirable. Further than that, authorities beg to differ. I try everything from sticking it in the oven with no more than a coat of salt, as suggested by Delia, to the Chinese-duck-style treatment espoused by Simon Hopkinson, who has me scalding, air-drying and salting like Ken Hom himself, but the clear winner is, obviously, the slightly nutty recipe suggested by food blogger Gastronomy Domine. In an effort to dry the meat out as much as possible, she treats it to a rub down, gives it the once-over with a hairdryer, and leaves it in the fridge overnight, covered only with a tea towel, until the skin is as desiccated as an old camel bone in the Kalahari – then, and only then, is it ready for the oven. (The fridge is a very dry environment, which is why it's best not to store bread in there.)

Great crackling seems to require three things: a bone-dry rind — and you can't beat a hairdryer for this — generous levels of salt, and a quick blast in a blisteringly hot oven, in accordance with the teachings of Hugh Fearnley-Whittingstall. Adding extra fat, as *Good Housekeeping* does, is an unnecessary decadence.

To rescue disappointing crackling, carefully detach it from the meat and stick it in the microwave for a couple of minutes, to give it a texture reminiscent of a porky Aero — not ideal, but better than admitting defeat, and far superior to popping it under a hot grill, which, in defiance of all logic, does disappointingly little for the texture.

1 joint of pork with a generous coating of fat
Salt

1. The day before you want to eat the pork, score the skin with a sharp knife if your butcher hasn't already done so — cut a regular diamond pattern into the fat, but don't go as far down as the meat. Pat the joint dry with kitchen paper, and rub vigorously with salt. Now, take a hairdryer, and gently blow-dry the joint until the skin is absolutely dry — you'll feel ridiculous, but it's worth it, I promise. If you don't own a hairdryer, you need to be extra diligent with the paper towels. Cover the joint with a tea towel and put into the fridge overnight.
2. On the day itself, preheat the oven to 220°C/425°F/gas 7, take the joint out of the fridge, and rub some more salt into the skin. Put it into a roasting tin (you can add sliced onions, herbs, garlic — whatever flavourings you fancy — into the tin as well) and roast for half an hour, then turn down the heat to

170°C/325°F/gas 3 and roast for 35 minutes per 450g until the juices run clear.

3. Check the crackling – if it isn't quite crisp enough for your liking, you can very carefully cut it from the joint and put it back into the oven for another few minutes – turn it up as high as it will go, and keep an eye on it.

4. Take the meat out of the oven and allow to rest in a warm place for at least 20 minutes before carving.

Perfect
Fish Pie

Who says beige is boring? Fish pie, with its kaleidoscope of off-white hues, is delicious proof that food doesn't have to be all the colours of the Mediterranean rainbow to beguile. Just thinking about it on a cold day can make me feel all warm and fuzzy inside – so it's worth making two and keeping one in the freezer for comfort food emergencies.

A word about that seductive golden top – Angela Boggiano uses a pastry crust for her smoked fish and cider pie, and Nigel Slater suggests a most unorthodox crumble, but for sheer comfort you can't beat a cloud of fluffy mash. In homage to J. Sheekey, purveyors of the finest fish pies in London, I've topped mine with a few breadcrumbs to give it a bit of crunch. Adding cheese to a properly seasoned mash is de trop as far as I'm concerned, but you can follow their example and sprinkle over a little Parmesan if you're feeling decadent.

A firmly traditional white sauce is the backbone of Nigel's crumble-crust fish pie; it's comfortingly thick, but I prefer the flavour of Marco Pierre White's gorgeously savoury fish stock reduction with double cream. As a compromise, I retain the texture of the white sauce, but add a bit more flavour by using wine and stock to poach the fish instead, in homage to Tom Aikens' recipe.

Jamie Oliver includes a characteristically unorthodox recipe using a double cream, mustard and cheese sauce in *The Return of the Naked Chef*, which, while admittedly delicious, utterly overpowers the delicate flavour of the fish. (He also puts the fish in raw, which makes the pie a bit watery, as it gives off liquid as it cooks.) I've gone for more subtle flavourings: parsley adds a fresh note, and a little anchovy salty richness, but I do like his use of spinach — I often put in a few handfuls, or some sautéd leeks, to bulk out the filling.

Serve with plenty of steamed greens to mop up the creamy sauce — anything else is overkill.

Serves 4

- 1kg floury potatoes (e.g. Maris Piper or King Edward)
- Salt and pepper
- 50g butter
- 100ml milk
- 350g white fish and/or salmon fillets
- 350g smoked white fish
- 500ml homemade fish stock (see page 174) or ready-made stock (but not cubes)
- 100ml dry white wine
- A small bunch of flat-leaf parsley, separated into leaves (finely chopped) and stalks
- 50g butter
- 50g plain flour

100ml double cream
2 anchovy fillets in oil, drained
  and finely chopped
200g small peeled prawns
25g white breadcrumbs

1. Peel the potatoes and cut into evenly sized chunks. Put into a
    large pan, cover with cold water, add a generous pinch of salt,
    and bring to the boil. Simmer for about 20 minutes, until
    tender. Drain, allow to sit in the colander for a few minutes,
    then mash until smooth, beating in the butter and a splash of
    milk. Season well and set aside.
2. Preheat the oven to 180°C/350°F/gas 4. Remove any skin from
    the fish and check for bones. Strain the stock to get rid of any
    floating bits of fish or skin, then put into a large pan with the
    wine and parsley stalks and bring to a simmer. Add the fish,
    simmer for a couple of minutes, then lift out with a slotted
    spoon and cut into large chunks. Discard the parsley stalks.
3. Melt the butter in a medium pan over a lowish heat, and stir in
    the flour. Cook, stirring, for a couple of minutes, being careful
    not to let it brown. Gradually stir in the stock. Bring to the
    boil, then simmer very gently for about 20 minutes, stirring
    frequently.
4. Take the sauce off the heat, stir in the double cream, chopped
    parsley leaves and anchovies and season. Add the fish and prawns
    and toss to coat.
5. Put the seafood and sauce into a large baking dish (30 x 28cm
    would be ideal) and top with the mashed potato. Bake for 20
    minutes, then sprinkle over the breadcrumbs and bake for a
    further 20 minutes, until the top is golden brown.

TIP

----

5 fish to eat and 5 fish to avoid
Nearly half the fish eaten in the UK is from just
three species: cod, salmon and tuna — what an
unadventurous lot we are. Not only is this downright
dull, but it's putting undue pressure on stocks, so
next time you're making a fish pie, stick something
new in there. You never know, you might even enjoy
it. Visit www.fishonline.org for the full list.

Eat
Grey or red gurnard
Cornish sardines
Dab
Sprats
Pollock

Avoid
Bluefin tuna
Wild turbot
Dogfish/rock salmon
Eel
Skate

Perfect
Fishcakes

*P*roof, if any were needed after the pie, that seafood and potato go
together like Sharky and George. I've long been a secret fan of those
day-glo curling stones served in chippies, but I really fell in love
with fishcakes on my eighteenth birthday, when a boyfriend of the
time whisked me to lunch at Le Caprice. Ah, the heady taste of
house white, fishcakes and sorrel sauce, with Dame Judi Dench at
the next table.

Fishcakes don't have to be grand, though — as Simon Hopkinson and
Lindsey Bareham point out in their recipe in *The Prawn Cocktail Years*,
they're often the resort of leftover fish, and none the worse for that.
As you're only heating the cakes through, the ingredients all need to
be pre-cooked, making them the perfect vehicle for that cold bit of
salmon or morsel of smoked mackerel. They use crushed potato
rather than the more traditional mash, which gives the fishcakes a
more interesting texture, but you don't need the double cream in
their recipe, unless you're after a particularly rich result. The same
goes for the melted butter in gastropub stalwart Trish Hilferty's
Lobster & Chips recipe: a humble egg should be binding enough. Chill
before use to firm them up, or you'll end up
with a fish hash instead. Still
delicious, but less likely to
impress your guests.

Flavourings are up to you — I tried out spring onion, hard-boiled egg, parsley and chopped gherkins before deciding on capers and anchovies, which add the salt and vinegar that's all the seasoning you need with fish and potatoes. Although Le Caprice simply coat their fishcakes in flour before frying, I like the crunch of breadcrumbs; perhaps it reminds me of the chippie. Serve with sautéd spinach.

Serves 2

400g floury potatoes
   (e.g. Maris Piper)
Salt and pepper
250g fish: salmon, firm white
   fish or smoked haddock work
   particularly well
1 tablespoon chopped chives
1 tablespoon capers
2 anchovy fillets in oil, drained
   and finely chopped
1 egg, beaten
40g flour, for coating
50g fresh white breadcrumbs
A generous knob of butter
1 tablespoon vegetable oil

1. Peel the potatoes and cut into evenly-sized chunks. Put into a large pan and cover with cold water. Add a generous pinch of salt and bring to the boil, then turn down the heat slightly and simmer until tender, but not mushy. Drain and put back into the hot pan for a minute to dry off, then roughly crush

them with a fork, so they're a mixture of mash and larger lumps.

2. Meanwhile, put the fish into a large pan and just cover with water. Bring to a simmer, then gently cook for 3–5 minutes, depending on the size of the fillets, until the skin, if any, pulls off easily, and it's just beginning to flake. Drain and set aside to cool, then skin if necessary, break into large flakes and add to the potatoes.

3. Stir in the chives, capers and anchovies. Season lightly, and mix together gently, adding a little of the beaten egg to bring the mixture together into patties – it shouldn't be too sloppy. Use your hands to form into four large cakes or six smaller ones.

4. Put the remaining egg in a shallow bowl, and tip the flour and breadcrumbs on to separate saucers. Dip each fishcake in turn into the flour, the egg, and finally the breadcrumbs until thoroughly coated. Put into the fridge for at least half an hour to firm up.

5. Heat a frying pan with the butter and oil until the butter begins to foam. Add the fishcakes, in batches if necessary, cook for 5 minutes on a medium-high heat until golden and well crusted, then turn them carefully over and repeat on the other side.

How to tell if your fish is fresh
First off, unless you're buying farmed fish like salmon or trout, avoid buying fish on a Monday – fishing boats don't go out on a Sunday. The rest of the week, don't be afraid to get up close and personal with your prospective dinner when giving it the once-over – fresh fish should smell of the

sea, so any unpleasant 'fishy' odours are bad news. Look for clear rather than cloudy eyes on whole fish, and shiny, slick skin or a full complement of bright scales. Fillets should look wet — if they feel dry, or are already flaking apart, they're probably not fit for anyone but the cat.

Perfect
Kedgeree

*I*f anything good came out of the British occupation of India, it's food. (For us, that is; India got railways, slightly less excitingly.) Like chicken tikka masala, kedgeree is a prime example of a culinary mash-up, and is the best cure for a hangover I know — if you feel well enough to make it, that is.

I don't think cream's desirable here — it dulls the flavours of the 'wet kedgeree' recipe from *The Prawn Cocktail Years*, and this is a dish that demands a bit of spice. After all, the Empire wasn't built on porridge alone. The fishless recipe in the 1888 collection *The Complete Indian Cook and Housekeeper* (reproduced in the utterly fascinating study of the British love affair with curry, *The Road to Vindaloo*) calls for the rice to be simmered in water, rather like a plain paella — it's tasty enough, but nothing like kedgeree as we know it. Cooking the rice in the fish poaching liquid is a nice idea from Jane Grigson, but again, it seems to make the dish less vivid; the *Leiths Fish Bible* version, which is more of a fish fried rice, enlivened with generous amounts of butter, gives the most satisfying result. Sautéing pre-cooked rice in curry powder (this is one recipe where that strangely old-fashioned spice mix is absolutely appropriate) keeps the flavours fresh, and the texture firm, rather than mushy, to make a breakfast dish that leaves you in no doubt that you're alive and well.

Leiths include fresh ginger, which I don't really like with the smoked haddock, but the green chilli adds a nice freshness to the dish – if you can't take too much heat in the mornings, you can leave it out. I sometimes substitute chopped coriander for the chives, particularly later in the day – this also, of course, makes a great supper dish.

Serves 4

500g smoked haddock
120g butter
1 large onion, finely chopped
1 green chilli, deseeded and cut
   into thin rings
2 cardamom pods, lightly crushed
1 tablespoon medium curry powder
200g basmati rice, cooked (see page 93)
2 large free-range eggs, hard-boiled,
   peeled and cut in half (see page 2)
15g chives, finely chopped
½ a lemon, cut into 4 wedges

1. Put the fish, skin-side up, in a shallow pan over a low heat, and cover with boiling water. Poach for 10 minutes, then take out of the water and, when cool enough to handle, pull the skin off, remove any bones and break into large flakes.
2. Melt the butter in a large frying pan over a lowish heat, and add the onion. Cook gently for 20 minutes until softened, then stir in the chilli, cardamom pods and curry powder. Cook for a further 5 minutes, then tip in the rice and heat through for 2–3

minutes, stirring to coat. Add the fish flakes and heat through. Taste and season.

3. Put the eggs on top, scatter with chives, and serve with wedges of lemon to squeeze over.

Perfect
Prawn Cocktail

After years languishing in the doldrums of naffness, this classic
60s starter has enjoyed a small renaissance of late, largely thanks to
our national passion for nostalgia – and Marie Rose sauce. This,
of course, is the element on which the dish's flimsy integrity stands
or falls, which is why I'd urge making homemade mayonnaise the
backbone. Nigella reckons salad cream works like a dream, but I
found it made the sauce rather vinegary, and adding mascarpone,
as suggested by a recipe on the Waitrose website, seemed to serve
no discernible purpose except for selling more cheese. Keep it
firmly trad.

You don't want to muck around too much with the
flavourings either – as Nigel Slater points out. Tomato
ketchup (Simon Hopkinson and Lindsey Bareham say
it has to be Heinz, and as they named a book after the
dish, they must know a thing or two about it) is a
must; tomato chutney, as used by *Good Food*,
just doesn't give the same wonderful sweet and sour flavour. Tabasco,
that stalwart of the veneer cocktail cabinet, provides a subtle kick, and
a dash of brandy suggests true 1960s sophistication. That, and a dash
of lemon juice, is really all you need: Delia's Worcestershire sauce
takes over the party (in fact, in combination with prawn cocktail, it
reminds me powerfully of swapping crisps in the playground), and her
lime adds a jarring freshness to the cosily retro flavours. Again, don't
try to be too clever; this is not a dish which needs fixing.

Little gem lettuces are a favourite here, but this is perhaps the only occasion for which I reckon iceberg is a must (other possibilities include hamburgers, and tacos – in fact, come to think of it, they deserve a revival too). The very blandness that renders iceberg so pointless in a salad is a boon here – stronger flavours, like watercress or, God forbid, rocket, would compete with the cocktail sauce – and it adds a pleasingly crunchy counterpoint to the softness of the prawns. I've stolen the idea of green pepper from a relative, who turns up every Christmas with the best prawn cocktail I have ever tasted: that herbaceous slight bitterness works wonderfully with the sweetness of the ketchup. Avocado is also a nice touch if you're feeling decadent – it takes the dish into the 1970s, which is about as far as you want to go before you hit the sun-dried tomatoes.

Serves 4

5 tablespoons mayonnaise
   (see page 150)
¼ of a green pepper, finely chopped
1 tablespoon tomato ketchup
1 teaspoon brandy
Tabasco sauce
½ a lemon
Salt and pepper
400g peeled prawns
½ iceberg lettuce, finely shredded
½ a cucumber, diced
A small handful of chives,
   finely chopped
Cayenne pepper, to serve

1. Mix the mayonnaise with the green pepper, ketchup and brandy and add a couple of drops of Tabasco and a squeeze of lemon. Season, taste and adjust if necessary. Toss with the prawns.

2. Divide the lettuce and cucumber between 4 serving dishes, then spoon the prawns on top and drizzle any extra sauce over them. Sprinkle with chives and dust with a little cayenne pepper.

Perfect
Moules Marinière

Moules marinière has become a bit of a catch-all term for any big bowl of mussels, but *marinière* is, in fact, the name of a white wine and shallot sauce which can be used to cook all manner of seafood – and, according to *Larousse Gastronomique*, even frogs.

Up in Normandy, they often make their marinières with local cider and cream – Lucas Hollweg of the *Sunday Times* has a recipe for this variation using leeks, but although it's delicious, cider sauces always make me think of roast pork.  Comparing seafood specialist Rick Stein's recipe, with its double cream, to a simpler one points up how dairy can dull flavours – it's lovely, in the way that anything with cream is lovely, but I'm struggling to pick up the mineral taste of mussels. I'll be opting for a simpler treatment, to make the seafood, rather than the sauce, the star – finishing the dish with butter, as Tom Aikens suggests, adds richness enough. You can also thicken the sauce with the butter at this point, as *Larousse* suggests, but I think this makes it too fussy – I prefer a lighter broth for dunking my baguette, and in any case, such a delay tends to make the mussels cold.

Simon Hopkinson and Lindsey Bareham use onion, rather than shallot, in their stripped-down recipe, but I like the sweeter, slightly vinous flavour of the smaller allium, even if it is impossible to emerge dry-eyed from any dealings with the things. I don't think you need garlic as well, it just seems like overkill in Tom Aikens' recipe. It's particularly important to use wine you'd be prepared to drink here, as moules marinière made with plonk will taste of just that. Muscadet, the bone-dry Loire white, makes an ideal companion for this dish, so use that and drink the rest. Look for that marked as *sur lie*, which will have a bit more weight to it.

Serves 2

2 shallots, finely chopped
2 sprigs of thyme, leaves picked
1 bay leaf
100ml dry white wine
1kg mussels, rinsed and with
   beards removed
50g butter
A small bunch of flat-leaf
   parsley, finely chopped

1. Put the shallots, thyme leaves, bay leaf and wine into a large pan and bring to a simmer. Cook for 10 minutes.
2. Put the mussels into the pan, cover and cook over a medium-high heat until the shells open, shaking occasionally to redistribute them: this should take about 3 minutes.
3. Add the butter and parsley, shake well and serve with a bowl for empty shells – discard any mussels which have remained closed during cooking.

How to store and clean mussels

Mussels are sold live, and need to be kept cool
and damp, but not wet. The bottom of the fridge,
covered with a damp tea towel, should be fine:
they'll be happy enough for twenty-four hours.
Before you use them, scrub them well to get rid
of any barnacles, and pull off the hairy 'beards'
they use to attach themselves to rocks. Mussels with
cracked shells, or which remain closed when tapped,
should be thrown away — it may seem a waste, but
better safe than sick as a dog.

Cooking with wine

The old adage, never cook with wine you wouldn't
be prepared to drink, is true — to an extent. Do you
really want the dominant flavour of your dish to be
thin and acidic, overpoweringly oaky, or just plain
off? Steer clear of anything marked cooking wine
for a start; it'll be overpriced rubbish. Saying that,
neither should you splash out on a Châteauneuf du
Pape, which Elizabeth David records one Nîmois
cook bringing out for a beef and olive stew in *French
Provincial Cooking* (in fact, simmering that kind of wine
for two hours might well be a prosecutable offence
across the Channel). Do try, however, to match the
strength and character of the wine to the dish. The
most versatile whites are clean and fresh-tasting —
avoid anything strongly oaky, or too aromatic: dry

white vermouth is a useful standby. Reds should be full-bodied and fruity, but not overpoweringly so: you don't want the sauce to be sweet, or tannic and bitter; depending on the dish, Beaujolais or Merlot are reliable choices.

CHAPTER 3

Rice, Pasta and Potatoes

These are the unsung heroes of the culinary world – the accompaniments that, in many cases, really make a dish. We may sing the praises of rare-breed sausages, but they wouldn't be half as good without their trusty sidekick of hot, fluffy mash – and how about a bolognese sauce without pasta? They can be unobtrusive accompaniments, or the star of a dish, a bowl of simply steamed rice, or a rich risotto – but these ingredients have nothing to hide behind, so make sure you get them right. From the most basic jacket potato, smashed open and garnished with butter, to the labour of love that is the twice-cooked chip, treat them with respect, and they'll be comfort food for life.

Perfect
Chips

*F*orget desiccated wedges, or the pallid crimes of burger joints:
proper chips should be thick-cut and defiantly potatoey: golden to
the eye, hot and fluffy within. Such perfection is not easily found
— particularly since the inexplicable rise of the loathsome Jenga
chip — but, with the basics mastered, it's easy enough to achieve at
home. Although there are always going to be times when only a
vinegary parcel from the Codfather, or a rustling pile of pommes
allumettes will do, a good chip recipe under your belt is surely a
friend for life.

The first thing to do is choose the ingredients. As there are only two
of them, this should, I used to think, be a breeze. I am not the first
to make this mistake: 'Unfortunately,' Hertfordshire gastropub chef
Paul Bloxham explains bitterly, 'the wrong potato will result in a
guaranteed failure.' Spuds divide neatly into two camps:
waxy, like Charlotte and Maris Peer, and floury, such
as King Edward and Maris Piper. Most recipes
call for the latter, but Heston Blumenthal,
who has, of course, looked into the
matter with a degree of thoroughness I
can only dream of, uses Charlotte or Belle
de Fontenay for what he describes as 'the best chips I have
ever tasted'. Although they produce a handsome golden chip,
however, I find them unacceptably dense. Maris Pipers it is.
Although it will make your kitchen smell like a chippie for weeks

afterwards, Mark Hix, who serves some pretty good fish and chips at his Dorset restaurant, is spot on with his observation that beef dripping gives a crisper and tastier chip than vegetable oil.

Rinsing the chips to wash off the starch, as Hix suggests, is a good idea, but soaking them in cold water, like the Hairy Bikers, makes them soggy. You then need to par-boil them – frying them from raw, as Randall & Aubin chef Ed Baines does, will leave them mahogany by the time they've cooked through – and chill them before the first and second frying. This may seem pointless, but Heston's done his research right – cooking them from cold really does give a crisper result, and what's a few more minutes where the perfect chip's concerned?

200g Maris Pipers per person
Dripping or other animal fat,
to cook (enough to half fill
your pan when melted)

You'll need a cooking thermometer, or an electric deep fat fryer, for this recipe.

1. Peel your potatoes and cut into chips – approximately 1cm for thick-cut chips, half that for thinner ones. Rinse well under cold water, then drain.
2. Put the chips into a pan of cold, salted water and bring to the boil. Turn down the heat, and simmer until just soft to the point of a knife.
3. Drain, pat dry and allow to cool, then put into the fridge until cold.
4. Heat your fat to 120°C, and add the chips. Don't overcrowd the

pan. Blanch for about 5 minutes, until cooked through but not coloured.

5. Remove, drain, pat dry, and refrigerate.
6. When you're ready to eat, heat the fat to 160°C and add the chips. Cook until crisp and golden, then remove, drain, season and serve immediately with plenty of salt.

Perfect
Pasta

Garibaldi relied on the power of macaroni to unite Italy, Sophia
Loren famously claimed she owed her voluptuous figure to spaghetti
– and the chef Giorgio Locatelli reckons every Italian is two-thirds
pasta. Despite a lingering fondness for 'hoops', even Britain has
embraced proper pasta in recent years. These days we know our
pappardelle from our penne; and we're beginning to get the concept
of different shapes for different sauces, but most of us still don't see
the point of making our own.

Dried pasta and fresh egg pasta are two different
beasts. You wouldn't use a waxy potato for baking,
for the same reason an Italian wouldn't serve
dried spaghetti with a game ragù – it doesn't work.
Fresh egg pasta gets its 'bite' from the egg
proteins, and is traditionally served with the
butter, cream and rich meat dishes of the north,
while dried pasta generally pairs better with the
olive oil and tomato recipes of the south.

Good dried pasta is widely available these days, as long as you're
prepared to spend a bit more than you would on the budget
varieties, and, with a little practice, you can produce your own fresh
stuff which will knock the socks off anything from the supermarket
– a product which, as Locatelli says, has 'real personality'.

You need a mixture of plain flour – preferably finely milled (or '00' grade, as you might find it labelled by Italian brands) for a really silky texture – and semolina for pasta; if you just use '00', as in the River Café recipe, it won't be as interesting, and the sauce won't cling to the strands in the same way. The more eggs you mix with the flour, the crisper the result – but if you go overboard with the yolks, you'll get a pasta that's so rich it will compete with any sauce you put with it. Adding olive oil to the dough, as the part-Italian Michelin-starred chef Angela Hartnett does, seems to be gilding the linguine lily; you can't taste it, and it's out of keeping with the northern, butter-based sauces you should be pairing it with.

Real nonnas scorn pasta machines, and roll their dough out on a board using an enormous pin, but for amateurs and Brits, they're a useful tool. If you don't have one, however, cut your dough into quarters, and roll each one out as thinly as possibly before cutting it into strips – you can find videos showing the process online.

Folding the dough back on itself during the rolling-out process may seem like an unnecessary faff, but it does, as Angela observes, give a more elastic, uniform result in the end: you can't rush great ravioli.

When it comes to cooking your pasta, never, ever add oil to the water – not only does it not stop it sticking together in the pan (using a large pan, and agitating the pasta, should see to that), but it will make it more difficult for the sauce to cling to the pasta later. Tossing it together in the pan, rather than dolloping the sauce on top at the table, will also help with this. Don't skimp on the salt, though; a cavalier attitude to health is one of the reasons that pasta always tastes better in Italy.

Makes around 750g (enough for 6–8)

340g '00' flour
160g fine semolina flour
½ teaspoon fine sea salt
4 large free-range eggs and 2 egg
    yolks, at room temperature,
    lightly beaten

1. Mix the flours and the salt and shape into a volcano on the work
    surface, or a wooden board. Make a well in the middle, and pour
    in two-thirds of the eggs.
2. Using your fingertips in a circular motion, gradually stir in the
    flour until you have a dough you can bring together into a ball,
    adding more egg if necessary. Knead for about 10 minutes, until
    it is smooth and springs back when poked, wetting your hands
    with cold water if necessary.
3. Divide the dough in two and wrap in a damp cloth. Allow to rest
    for about an hour in a cool place.
4. With a rolling pin, roll out the first ball of dough on a lightly
    floured surface until it is about 1cm thick and will go through the
    widest setting of your pasta machine comfortably. Put it through a
    couple of times on the widest setting, folding it back on itself each
    time and using a small amount of flour to prevent it sticking. Roll
    through the pasta on the next setting down, then back up to the
    widest setting. Repeat this whole process a couple more times; this
    will work the dough and help it become more silky in texture. Then
    start working your way down, from the widest setting to the second
    narrowest. Cut the dough in half when it becomes too long to
    handle and finish one piece at a time, using small amounts of flour
    dredged over the dough to prevent sticking.

5. When the pasta has a good sheen to it, and is thin enough for your liking – pappardelle and tagliatelle should be cut on the second narrowest gauge, filled pastas such as ravioli on the narrowest – cut using a knife, or the cutter on your pasta machine. Curl into portion-sized nests and leave on a floured surface, under a damp cloth, while you repeat with the rest of the dough. Freeze any you're not going to use immediately – or leave it out on the counter overnight, under a tea towel, until completely dry, then store in an airtight container as you would any dried pasta.

6. Bring a large pan of well-salted water to the boil, add the pasta, in batches if necessary, and cook for a couple of minutes, stirring occasionally to keep it moving. Serve immediately.

Perfect
Rice

Given that it's the world's second most popular grain (pub quizzers: maize comes in at number one), and one that's been eaten in this country since medieval times, we're strangely content to be bad at cooking rice. Either it's served up in dry, claggy clumps, or – and perhaps worse – it's sliding sloppily across the plate in a trail of cooking water. Ugh.

Theories abound as to the best way to cook rice. Having never enjoyed much success with the microwave (watching food spin has  limited appeal, so I always end up cleaning up rice from the inside afterwards), and lacking the room for a dedicated rice cooker, it's the hob for me. The recipe below is for basmati, or other long-grain rices, the kind you might eat with a curry or make into a pilaff; short-grain and sticky rices will need rather different treatment.

Although the rice we buy in this country doesn't tend to need much washing, Madhur Jaffrey, the actress turned food writer who introduced many Britons to the idea of Indian home cooking in the 1960s and 70s, calls for it to be soaked before cooking. Annoying as this is when you remember it at the last minute, I've found it does help the grains stay separate, although if you don't have the time, it's not a disaster.

Given that rice tends either to be too dry, or too soggy, it's clearly important to get the ratio of water to rice right, rather than just chucking your 200g into an enormous pan of water and hoping for the best. Madhur Jaffrey helpfully gives a ratio of 1 part dry rice to 1½ parts water, which is simple enough to work out for any quantity of rice you might happen to be cooking.

Sri Owen, author of *The Rice Book*, one of the few single-subject books of the last twenty years worth the cover price, recommends bringing it to the boil, stirring once, then leaving it to simmer until all the water has been absorbed. So far so good – but the next stage, in which the rice is covered and cooked for another ten minutes over a very low heat, leaves me with distinctly sticky results, and a hard job washing up (her tip, which I read belatedly, about putting the pan on a wet tea towel after cooking is a useful one, however. It stops the rice sticking to the bottom of the pan).

Jamie Oliver claims his method for light and fluffy rice is foolproof – he boils it briefly, then transfers the rice to a colander and steams it over the pan of boiling water until it's cooked through. Personally, I think you'd be a fool to let yourself in for so much unnecessary washing up for something so simple.

Step forward Madhur, a woman who has some practice in making exotic foodstuffs simple for British cooks. She brings rice to the boil, then immediately turns down the heat and covers the pan. It's nerve-racking stuff – you can't take the lid off to peep before the twenty-five minutes are up, or you'll let the steam out – but as long as you get the measurements right, I guarantee it will work perfectly, leaving you plenty of time to get on with making the rest of the dinner. And if something does go wrong, console yourself with the knowledge that in rice-eating cultures around the world, from Iran

to Korea, that 'burnt' crust at the bottom of the pan is eagerly
fought over as a delicacy – in fact, in Puerto Rico, there are even a
number of popular *merengue* songs devoted to singing its praises.
Remember that as you're doing the washing up.

Serves 6

450g basmati rice
A pinch of salt

1. Toss the rice under running water for a minute and then put it
   into a large pan and cover with cold water. Leave for at least half
   an hour.
2. Drain the rice and discard the soaking water. Put it into a large
   pan on a medium heat with 585ml of fresh cold water and a
   generous pinch of salt.
3. Bring to the boil, and give it a good stir. Cover tightly and turn
   the heat down very low. Cook for 25 minutes, then take off the
   heat – don't take the lid off! – and place on a wet tea towel. Leave
   for 5 minutes, then fork through to fluff up.

Different kinds of rice
We tend to speak of rice as a single
ingredient when in fact there are
hundreds of varieties in use around
the world. However, once you've
discounted the parboiled parvenus
peddled by a certain elderly

gentleman, which are an affront to taste and decency, you'll be lucky to find more than a handful in your local shop – which is fine, as long as you know what to use them for.

Long-grain: Slim and pointy, these varieties are best for when you want fluffy rice to serve as a side dish, or separate grains for fried rice. Basmati, which hails from the foothills of the Himalayas, is the most prized kind – put your nose inside the packet to find out why. Jasmine rice, popular in Thailand, is another slightly stickier and less aromatic example.

Short-grain: Also known as pudding rice, this is used in Britain to denote a round, white rice which, when cooked, gives a sticky, starchy result, perfect for rice puddings. Obviously.

Risotto rice: Plump, starchy varieties such as Arborio, Carnaroli and Vialone Nano are essential for a really creamy risotto. You can also use them in a rice pudding, but the result will be slightly denser.

Sticky rice: Short-grained Asian rices which become sticky when cooked; often misleadingly known as glutinous rice, which simply refers to their glue-like consistency, as all rice is gluten-free. Also sold as sushi rice. Particularly popular in South-East Asia.

Brown rice: Minimally processed rice that retains more fibre, vitamins and minerals than polished white varieties, but which also takes longer to cook, and spoils faster. Any kind of rice may be sold as brown rice, but in this country it tends to denote long-grain.

Paella rice: Round-grained Spanish varieties such as Bomba and Calasparra. If you can't find them, substitute risotto rice instead.

Wild rice: The joker in the pack, wild rice is actually a grass, rather than a rice. It has a pleasant nutty flavour, and combines well with basmati.

Perfect
Risotto

*R*isotto recipes are always advertised as perfect for an 'easy, quick midweek supper' — a spurious claim that will only end in tears in the vast majority of cases. If you find yourself still miserably pushing around crunchy rice when you expected to be sitting down to eat, then it's easy to become disheartened and fry the bejeezus out of it instead. In fact, I've never had one on the table within half an hour, but if I can be so bold as to claim I finally understand the risotto, at least now I know why — which is much more satisfying.

First up, ingredients. Carnaroli rice is best — it's the least stodgy of the three main varieties, although if you can't find it, then either Arborio or Vialone Nano will be absolutely fine. The stock you use to cook it must be genuinely tasty — after all, it's going to be the predominant flavour of the dish — so this is a great midweek dish for using up the stock you've made from Sunday's roast chicken (see page 173). You also need a generous hand with the dairy at the end, because it's the *mantecare*, or beating in the butter and cheese, which gives the risotto that essential richness. As Nigella's favourite cookery writer, and the author of the wonderful 'memoir with food' *Risotto with Nettles*, Anna del Conte, so wisely says, if you don't want butter, eat something else. The finished risotto should ripple obligingly across the plate, instead of sitting in one grim, sticky lump.

The traditional way to make risotto is to toast the rice first, and then cook it in hot stock, adding just a little at a time, until you achieve the right texture. Constant stirring is also essential, as it releases the starches in the rice that give risotto its characteristic creamy consistency. All in all, it's a pretty labour-intensive process. Although I've experimented with various quick fixes, including food writer Richard Erlich's hands-off approach, which involves tipping in a good glug of stock and then leaving the dish to its own devices for a bit while you grate the cheese, or make a salad, and Parisian chef Toni Vianello's oven-cooked risotto (as recommended by no less a person than Simon Hopkinson), which relies on the *mantecare* for its creaminess, I find you can't beat the traditional method. Sadly.

Temperature is vital here: the onions should be cooked gently, so they soften without colouring, but it's crucial that the rice is hot when you add the wine, so turn up the heat to toast it unless you want to be at the stove all evening. The stock must also be hot for the same reason — whatever anyone says about finding stirring a risotto therapeutic, it gets very boring indeed after half an hour.

Once you've mastered the basic technique, you can play around with flavourings as you wish: Giorgio Locatelli's *Made in Italy* has the best collection of recipes I've found (*River Café Cook Book Two* also comes highly recommended in this department) but generally speaking, any ingredients you might think of pairing with pasta will sit happily in a risotto — delicate flavours work best though.

Serves 4

2 litres good stock – chicken,
   vegetable or fish, depending
   on your flavourings
I onion, finely chopped
100g butter
400g Carnaroli rice
125ml dry white wine
Flavourings of your choice,
   e.g. 400g sautéd mushrooms; a
   bunch of steamed asparagus, chopped;
   Ikg mixed cooked seafood
100g Parmesan, finely grated
Salt and pepper

1. Bring the stock to the boil in a large pan (if you're using ready-made stuff, bear in mind it's often very salty, so taste and water it down if necessary). Keep at a simmer.

2. Soften the onion with a knob of the butter for 15 minutes over a lowish heat in a heavy-bottomed, straight-sided pan, then add the rice. Turn up the heat, and stir to coat the grains with butter. When they are hot (about 2 minutes), add the wine, and keep stirring until this has evaporated. To make sure the pan is hot enough start by adding a drop of wine – if it doesn't sizzle, turn up the heat before you pour in the rest.

3. Start adding the stock, a ladleful at a time. Stir until each ladleful has nearly all been absorbed – the rice should always be sloppy, rather than dry – and then add another, and so on. Add any extra ingredients at some point during this time, depending on how robust they are – usually about 10 minutes in, but if you

have something which will break up or overcook easily, such as seafood, stir it through a few minutes before serving.

4. When the rice starts to soften, begin pouring in the stock in smaller amounts, and testing it regularly, for 20 minutes or until it is cooked to your liking. Then add the rest of the butter, and most of the grated cheese, and beat in with gusto until the risotto is rich and creamy. Check the seasoning, and serve immediately with the remaining cheese, or leave to stand for a couple of minutes if you prefer a thicker texture.

Perfect
Mash

When you're feeling a bit miserable, or sniffly, nothing warms the cockles like a big bowl of steaming mash — not the refined restaurant stuff beloved of the French, who show their ignorance of the true beauty of the dish by using waxy, rather than floury potatoes, but the fluffy clouds of comfort that are the British equivalent of congee, or rice and peas, or dhal. You know you've been abroad too long when you begin to dream of mash.

In the interests of broad-mindedness, I have, of course, tried using waxy Charlotte potatoes rather than my usual floury Maris Pipers or King Edwards, but although well flavoured, they're too dense for my perfect mash. I'm still not sure what Heston was thinking of, recommending them. It's important to put the potatoes into cold water and bring it to the boil, rather than dropping them straight into hot water, or they won't cook evenly and you'll end up with soggy, lumpy mash.

Butter is of course a must for mash (it's the only addition Marco Pierre White will countenance), but other flavouring ideas abound, from Gruyère and roasted garlic to Dijon mustard. Nigel Slater claims milk is optional, but I like the slight sweetness that it brings to the dish — cream, as favoured by Jamie Oliver, tends to make it too rich for my taste. Not as rich, of course, as Heston's mash, which contains half as much butter as potato, and requires an array of gadgets, including a thermometer for temperature-controlled cooking, and a ricer, to purée it into submission. If you think there's no such thing as too much butter, I urge you to give his recipe a try.

Although a potato ricer, a gadget much favoured by professional chefs, and which looks like an over-sized garlic press, undoubtedly gives a smoother result, I find a traditional potato masher is the secret to the fluffiest mash – take no notice of Delia's advice about using an electric whisk unless you want to repaint your kitchen with starch. You can, of course, leave the skins on if you like, but I'd save that for crushed new potatoes instead – there's a time and a place for wholesomeness, and it's not on a plate of sausage (the perfect sausage, of course, see page 48) and mash.

Serves 4

900g floury potatoes, peeled
Salt and pepper
100g butter, cut into cubes
50ml milk

1. Cut the potatoes in roughly equal sized pieces, and put into a large pan of cold, well-salted water. Bring to the boil, then turn down the heat and simmer until tender. Drain well, and put the potatoes back into the hot pan for a couple of minutes to dry off completely.
2. Put the butter into the pan and mash the potato until smooth – you'll need to put a bit of effort in, but you will have earned your mash by the end.

3. Pour in half the milk and beat well with a wooden spoon, then repeat with the rest. Season to taste, and serve immediately – possibly straight out of the pan.

Potato varieties
A spud isn't just a spud. Over eighty varieties are grown for sale in this country – and very few of them, sadly, come with much in the way of labelling, although you can't miss the purple Shetland Black vintage potato (floury, good boiled) or the Pink Fir Apple (waxy, ideal for salads). If you're not familiar with what's on offer, you could end up with entirely the wrong potato for the job. Disintegrating dauphinoise? You'll have an over-floury potato. Chewy chip? Too waxy, mate.

Common floury varieties: ideal for fluffy mash, chips, jacket or roast potatoes: King Edward, Maris Piper
All-rounders: can be used for mashing, but will also hold their shape when boiled: Desiree, Wilja, Estima
Common waxy varieties: dense and flavourful, ideal for potato salads or simply boiling: Charlotte, Maris Peer, Jersey Royal

How to store potatoes
Potatoes grow underground. Remember this light-shunning tendency when you unpack your next

bag – leave them out on the counter and they'll turn green, and green potatoes are bad news: bitter, and potentially toxic. Cut out any verdant bits before cooking, and resolve to store them in a dark, cool place in future: a cellar would be ideal, but a well-ventilated cupboard is fine. If you don't have room for them in a cupboard, you can purchase bags with black linings to store your spuds in: never leave them in plastic, because they'll sweat.

Perfect
Jacket Potatoes

Jacket potatoes are the ultimate winter convenience food – my modest circle of friends includes a lady who was sent to school with one wrapped in foil as a hand-warmer-cum-packed-lunch and a triathlete who eschews the pre-race energy bars and powders beloved of his fellow competitors in favour of a simple spud; easier to open, apparently. There's nothing like a foodstuff that comes with its own edible wrapping to make you feel all eco-minded.

Although it has been suggested that the name itself is rather *infra dig*, I reckon a jacket potato suggests a very particular sort of baked spud – any old potato can have a delectably fluffy interior, but it takes real skill to achieve that wonderfully crunchy skin as well. It's not something that can be rushed, which is presumably why most high-street potatoes are such damp squibs: this is a treat best cooked at home.

Floury varieties are a must here – and, as befitting such a humble dish, you don't need much else. Oiling, as suggested by the BBC's food website, gives a better colour, but no other discernible benefit, and brining, an idea from across the pond, is just a waste of good salt; there's only so much sodium chloride one spud can soak up, and the interior tastes disappointingly ordinary. I quite like the idea of brushing the potatoes with butter, or even bacon grease, during cooking, but although the results are good, it's messy work, and cools the oven down too. You can get a crisp skin without them.

A word about the oven while we're on the subject: after years of cooking her potatoes fast and furious, Delia turned her oven down to 190°C in pursuit of the perfect crunch — but I find Nigel Slater's vicious 220°C more effective in my own quest, along with a light dusting of coarse salt for flavour. Always prick your potato before cooking, by the way; it doesn't seem to have any detrimental effect on them, and it's good insurance against an unhappy evening of oven cleaning should a rogue spud go mad and explode while your back's turned. Trust me, you don't want to risk it.

Hearteningly, even the likes of the great Slater admit that sometimes potatoes just do their own thing — at which point you should turn to cheese, and lots of it.

1 floury potato per person
 (e.g. Maris Piper, King Edward)
About 20g coarse sea salt

1. Preheat your oven to 220°C/425°F/gas 7.
2. When the oven is up to temperature, wash the potatoes well, and prick each in a couple of places with a fork. Allow to dry slightly while you tip your salt into a shallow bowl. Roll each potato in the salt to give an even coating, and then place on the middle shelf of the oven, preferably directly on the rack.
3. Cook for around an hour, then give them a quick squeeze — the potato should just give, and the skin should be distinctly crisp. If not, leave them for 10 minutes, and check again — if you overcook them, the insides will be dry, so it's important to be vigilant.

4. Take out of the oven and put whole on to plates: they shouldn't be opened until you're ready to eat, and then preferably by hitting them sharply so they burst, for maximum fluffiness — you can cover your hand with a tea towel to do this if you're feeling wimpy, but remember, sometimes you have to suffer for perfection. Do your thing with butter, and tuck in immediately.

Perfect
Roast Potatoes

*T*he meat may be the nominal centrepiece of a Sunday roast, but if you get your roast potatoes right then frankly, you could serve chicken nuggets and most people would still be happy as Larry. There's no big secret to greatness here: you don't need to dust them with semolina, as Nigella does (too grainy), or toss them in seasoned flour, as recommended by *Good Food* magazine. Don't boil them to the point of disintegration like Heston – there's no need, and half of them will fall apart – but do add some of the peelings to the pan when parboiling; you might feel like a fool, but they really do improve the flavour (just taste the cooled water for the proof). All you really need is hot fat, and an even hotter oven. And, of course, floury potatoes – waxy ones will never fluff up properly.

As I said, the fat is important: beef dripping is good with beef and lamb, olive oil is surprisingly good (although I wouldn't bother with Michael Caine's recipe – the *Italian Job* star revealed on Radio 4's *Desert Island Discs* that restaurant critic and erstwhile filmmaker Michael Winner thinks he makes the best roast potatoes in the world but I found cooking them in a vat of cold extra virgin too greasy: use ordinary olive oil, preheated in the oven, instead) – but goose fat, if you're up for splashing out, gives the best flavour of all, and is ideal with pork and poultry. Make sure you get it nice and hot before you add the potatoes, and toss them in the fat before putting them into a good hot oven for at least 45 minutes – by the time they're ready, the meat should have rested and carved. There's no need to laboriously scrape them with a fork as Jane Grigson suggests: shaking them gently in the pan after boiling and draining should rough up the edges nicely.

Serves 6

This recipe also works for 450g of parsnips — blanch for 3 minutes instead, and cook for about 45 minutes

1.2kg floury potatoes (e.g. King Edward, Maris Piper)
Salt and pepper
2 tablespoons goose fat or 4 tablespoons olive oil

1. Preheat the oven to 190°C/375°F/gas 5. Wash and peel the potatoes, reserving the peel. Cut them into halves or quarters, depending on their size. Put them into a large pan of salted boiling water, along with the peel — it's easiest if you can put this in a muslin infusing bag. Parboil for 8 minutes.
2. Meanwhile, put 2 tablespoons of goose or duck fat or dripping, or 4 tablespoons of olive oil, into a roasting tin and put it into the oven to heat. Drain the potatoes and discard the peel, then put them back into the pan and shake gently to rough up the edges. Take the roasting tin out of the oven and put it on the hob over a medium heat. Put the potatoes in one by one — they should sizzle as they hit the pan — and baste all over. Season.
3. Roast for about an hour, until golden and crunchy, keeping an eye on them and basting with a little more fat if they begin to look dry.

Perfect
Yorkshire Puddings*

You can't beat a Yorkshire pud – in fact, everyone loves them so much I suspect that, with a decent gravy (see page 166), they could be revived as a thrifty way to pad out the joint in these straitened times. After all, who can keep their mind on meat if there's a crisp piece of billowing batter coming down the table in their direction?

I used to think you could only make a good Yorkshire if you'd got northern blood, but it turns out that's just plain daft. In fact, the only secret is heat, and lots of it – you need a smoking hot pan, and a blisteringly hot oven. That said, there's a few things you can do to make your puddings even prouder. For a start, use a metal, rather than a silicone tray; that way you can keep it warm on the stovetop while you ladle the batter in, and it also seems to help get those bottoms nice and crunchy.

If all this talk of crunch is puzzling, you probably hail from below the Watford Gap – according to the *Oxford Companion to Food*, us softie southerners prefer our batter puddings . . . well, a bit softer. However, up north they like their puddings to be crisp on the outside, and tender within, which is why I use Delia's mixture of milk and water for ultimate crunch, rather than celebrity chef James Martin's milk-only recipe, which gives a slightly sweeter, softer result (some Yorkshireman he is).

---

* A wildcard in a chapter devoted to pasta, potatoes and rice admittedly, but how could I leave them out?

Allowing the mixture to rest before cooking seems to give a more satisfactory result, although I couldn't see any benefit in adding the flour at the last minute, as the winner of the 1970 Great Yorkshire Pudding Contest apparently did. I reckon the real secret of his success was the number of eggs in his recipe, recorded for posterity by Jane Grigson in *English Food*.

Traditionally, Yorkshire puddings would have been cooked using the drippings from the roast – and, despite experimenting with Hugh's olive oil, and goose fat, as per the Hairy Bikers, I still think beef dripping gives the best flavour. It should be so hot that the batter sizzles as it hits the pan – put them straight into the oven, and don't open it for at least twenty minutes, because they're not quite as amenable as soufflés.

Once the puddings are cooked, serve them as soon as possible; you can put them in a low oven for a while if the rest of the meal isn't quite ready, but don't leave them sitting in a draught, or you'll have to pass them off as Staffordshire oatcakes. Canadian Susan Sampson reckons you should pierce the puddings as they leave the oven to let the steam out, but this didn't seem to do anything but make them a bit cold. Oh, and the name of the chef who won that competition? Mr Tin Sung Chan of Hong Kong. Turns out you really don't have to hail from God's own country to make a right fine pudding.

Makes 1 large pudding or 12 individual ones

250g plain flour
Salt and pepper
4 large free-range eggs

150ml whole milk

2 tablespoons beef dripping or sunflower oil

1. Sift the flour into a mixing bowl with a generous pinch of salt, then make a well in the middle and crack in the eggs. Mix the milk with 150ml of cold water, then pour a little in with the eggs and whisk in the flour to a smooth batter. Mix in the rest of the liquid; you should have a consistency much like that of single cream. Leave at room temperature for at least 15 minutes.

2. Once the meat has come out of the oven, turn it up to 230°C/450°F/gas 8 (this is probably the point where your roast potatoes should be just about done, so make sure they aren't going to burn in the next 20 minutes). Put a large roasting tray, or a muffin tin, with a couple of tablespoons of dripping in the bottom, on to a high shelf – there should be enough fat to grease, but the puddings shouldn't be swimming in them, so don't go overboard. Leave for 10 minutes to heat up.

3. Take the tin out of the oven and keep warm on the hob, if possible, while you ladle in the batter, which should sizzle as it hits the fat. Put back into the oven and cook for 15–20 minutes, until magnificently puffed up and golden. Keep an eye on the pudding or puddings towards the end, but don't be tempted to open the oven door until they're seriously bronzed, and you're just about to eat, as they will sink as they cool.

Toad in the Hole

To turn your Yorkshire pudding into that underrated school dinner favourite, toad in the hole, set the oven to 230°C/450°F/gas 8 and

 make your batter while it heats. Put 6 sausages into a greased roasting tin large enough to hold the pudding and cook for 15 minutes, then take out of the oven and put on the hob over a medium heat — the sausages should have released some fat, but if the tin looks dry, add 1 tablespoon of vegetable oil. When it's beginning to sizzle, add the batter, then return the tin to the oven and cook for 25 minutes. Serve with onion gravy.

CHAPTER 4

Vegetables and Pulses

We all know we should be eating more vegetables – but sometimes it's hard to find the inspiration to do them justice. In fact, they're remarkably forgiving as a food group, and, generally speaking, are extremely good value, which makes vegetable cookery a very useful skill to master. In her 1961 magnum opus *Mastering the Art of French Cooking*, Julia Child claims that the reason French vegetables taste better than our own is that they're interested in them as food, rather than just as a source of vitamins and minerals – a fact confirmed by Jane Grigson, who says that, for the majority of the British population, vegetables retained their essentially medicinal character until well after the Second World War, when they were liberated by the Mediterranean tastes of Elizabeth David and her ilk.

The collected works of David, and Grigson's *Vegetable Book*, first published in 1978, continue to be a reliable source of ideas today, but Italian and Indian cookery books are also great sources of enthusiasm – both cuisines recognize the potential of the vegetable kingdom to take centre stage, rather than acting as a dull supporting player. Buy local and in season, where possible — there's lot of information online as to what's best when, but you'll also be able to tell just by looking at what's cheapest and most abundant at any one time (with the exception of things like asparagus, which is pricey all year round, but oh-so worth it for those few weeks in early summer when it comes into season in this country). Root vegetables should be your friend in the winter — learn to love the ugly — and salads and more Mediterranean-style ingredients while the weather suits them; a fresh tomato in January is not worth the fuel it's flown in on.

Perfect
Leek and Potato Soup

American cookery legend Julia Child sums up the joys of this dish perfectly: it smells nice, tastes nice, and is 'simplicity itself' to make — a recipe worth committing to memory. I think the secret of this classic soup's comfort factor lies in the spuds: they give it a hearty, velvety texture that coats the throat like a warm muffler. Happily, leeks are in season from November to April — which just happens to be the time of year you're most likely to fancy a piping hot bowl of this.

Although the ingredients are humble, I think it's important to be generous with the butter: the water-based recipe in Lindsey Bareham's *A Celebration of Soup* is as plain as plain can be, and by God it tastes it. That said, unless you're making it for a special occasion, I don't think there's any need to add any milk or cream to the soup itself, as Darina Allen does; it dulls the flavour of the vegetables, which should be the stars of the show. As for Nigel Slater's Parmesan rinds, simmered until every ounce of flavour has seeped out into the broth — there are very few places in life where cheese isn't welcome, but this rustic, yet surprisingly subtle soup is one of them. Save it for the minestrone.

I am with Nigel, however, on the importance of slow-cooking the leeks in butter until they're 'silkily tender'; it really makes a difference to the finished flavour (and as Delia so wisely says, butter and leeks do have a peculiar affinity). He uses vegetable stock, which is fine, but I think a light chicken stock, as recommended in the Ballymaloe recipe, gives a more harmonious result – so many vegetable stocks are assertively herby, which is not what you want here.

Delia, who describes the soup as one of her own 'top of the pops favourites' on her website, suggests using discs of frozen mash instead of raw potato, which does speed the process up, but is prone to sticking to the pan, and gives a thinner consistency than I'm after. Pondering the potato element of the recipe, however, inspires me to make a soup using unpeeled spuds – these give it an undeniably more rustic appearance, but impart an earthy note reminiscent of jacket potatoes. Cosy.

To turn this into a simple vichyssoise, peel the potatoes, and add enough single cream to the finished soup to give a more elegant, light consistency – you'll probably need about 200ml. Stir in and chill before serving.

Serves 4

    3 fat leeks
    40g butter
    3 medium floury potatoes
    700ml chicken or vegetable stock
    Salt and pepper
    A small bunch of chives, chopped, to serve
    Single cream, to serve

1. Trim the leeks of their coarse green tops and slice. Rinse well under running water, then drain thoroughly. Melt the butter in a large, heavy-based pan over a low heat, and add the leeks. Season, cover, and sweat for 15 minutes, stirring occasionally to prevent them sticking.
2. Scrub the potatoes and cut into chunks – you only need to peel them if the skins are particularly dirty or blemished. Add to the leeks and cook for 5 minutes.
3. Cover the vegetables with stock and bring to a simmer. Partially cover the pan and leave to simmer gently for 45 minutes, until the potatoes have softened completely.
4. Blend until smooth, using a hand blender or liquidizer, then check the seasoning. Reheat and serve with a pinch of chopped chives and a swirl of cream.

Perfect
Gazpacho

*U*s Brits have long been suspicious of chilled soups – they seem unnatural somehow, in a climate more suited to tartan vacuum flasks and steaming broths. But just as we've taken tapas to our hearts and embraced the pungent joys of goat's cheese and garlic, we've grudgingly come to see the virtues of a cool, liquid lunch in our occasional warm spells.

Elizabeth David quotes the nineteenth-century French writer Théophile Gautier on gazpacho: 'At home, a dog of any breeding would refuse to sully its nose with such a compromising mixture.' But the 'hell-broth' works its magic even on this superior Parisian: 'strange as it may seem the first time one tastes it,' he continues, 'one ends by getting used to it and even liking it.' And so it is with us. The gazpacho is a classic of the genre, refreshing, and full of ripe, summery flavours; Lindsey Bareham's description of it as 'a salad soup' in *A Celebration of Soup* is absolutely spot on. It is, essentially, an Andalusian peasant dish designed to stretch cheap ingredients to their absolute limit.

The recipe for a classic gazpacho is fairly flexible, the main bone of contention being the inclusion of bread. Although bread has been a standard ingredient since the soup's medieval inception, Elizabeth David, in her *Mediterranean Food*, gives a recipe without it although including a number of less common ingredients such as chopped olives and marjoram, but I find that without it, the soup is thin, like a rather half-hearted salsa. Soaking the bread beforehand, as dictated by the wife of the former Spanish Ambassador to London, Elena Meneses de Orozco, seems to give the finished soup a better consistency, although I can't fathom why, given she then demands the bread be squeezed before use.

Lindsey wants me to peel the tomatoes, but as it all gets blended together eventually, I can't really see the point of this either — this is a pretty rustic soup, after all. Nor should ripe tomatoes need Gordon Ramsay's tomato purée — there's no point making this with anything but obscenely ripe ingredients. Anaemic midwinter tomatoes or crunchy peppers just won't cut the mustard when they're the stars of the show: you really will have to seek out good ingredients to make this worth your while. I like Señora Meneses' addition of green peppers, which give a pleasingly herbaceous flavour, but dismiss her cumin seeds, and Elizabeth David's black olives, as well as any sort of onion — they seem out of place in such a fresh-tasting dish, although you can always add them as a garnish later.

The real secret to gazpacho, if we assume your ingredients are ripe and your fridge cold, is good olive oil, and lots of it. Meanness has no place here, unless you're a frugal peasant — pour it in in great glugs, and then add vinegar to taste — sherry is the best, as gazpacho is an Andalusian dish, but red wine vinegar will do at a pinch. Don't be tempted to chill the soup with ice cubes, you'll just dilute the flavours — make it well ahead instead, so it has time to chill before serving. Choose your garnishes with care — mint is deliciously refreshing, olives add a nicely rich, savoury element to the clean flavours of the vegetables — and please, insist that everyone tries it before they make their excuses about cold soup.

Serves 4

1kg very ripe tomatoes, diced
1 ripe red pepper and 1 green
    pepper, deseeded and diced, plus
    ½ a ripe red pepper, cut into fine
    dice, to garnish
1 large cucumber, ¾ peeled and diced,
    ¼ washed and cut into fine dice, to garnish
2 cloves of garlic, peeled and crushed
150ml extra virgin olive oil, plus extra to serve
100g slightly stale crusty white bread,
    soaked in cold water for 20 minutes
Salt and pepper
2 tablespoons sherry vinegar
A small bunch of mint, leaves finely chopped, to garnish

1. Mix the diced tomatoes, peppers and cucumber with the crushed garlic and olive oil in the bowl of a food processor or blender. Squeeze out the bread, tear it roughly into chunks, and add to the bowl. Blend until smooth.

2. Pass the mixture through a sieve, pushing through as much as possible, then cover and refrigerate until well chilled. You will need to do this in batches.

3. Add salt, pepper and vinegar to taste, and stir well.

4. Spoon the chilled soup into bowls. Put a teaspoon of finely diced cucumber and red pepper, and a teaspoon of chopped mint, in the centre of the soup and circle with olive oil. For a more substantial dish, try adding any of the following: 2 hard-boiled eggs, peeled and chopped (see page 2), 2 slices of Serrano ham, cut into strips, or 1 tablespoon of black olives, stoned and finely chopped.

Perfect
Minestrone

Until recently, I thought I didn't like minestrone. This opinion was based solely on the strangely tangy powdered stuff, studded with suet-like strands of pasta, which was often the least-awful item on the school lunch menu. When the competition was stiffer than kidney stew, however, minestrone went out the window. Then I read Giorgio Locatelli on the subject – and discovered that, strictly speaking, minestrone isn't a *zuppa* at all, it's a kind of vegetable stew, with a few ladlefuls of broth on top, which makes it sound a lot more attractive. As Angela Hartnett observes, it should be a meal in itself.

In fact, as Locatelli and others point out, minestrone is more of a concept than a recipe, using whatever vegetables and thickeners happen to be available: courgettes, broad beans and peas in the spring, potatoes, chard and carrots in the winter. Common thickeners include broken bits of pasta, potato, beans, farro and rice – having tried all of them, I like to include cubes of potato, beans and risotto rice (at home, Locatelli admits he often makes a soup so thick with rice that his daughter can stand a spoon up in it – just as his grandmother did for him).

The really important thing to get right is the liquid which underpins the whole dish. Jamie comes down in favour of ham stock, while Locatelli uses vegetable stock for his light spring minestrone, and

Angela says chicken stock gives the best flavour, although she concedes one can also use vegetable at a pinch. Chicken is certainly the most versatile option; more subtle than ham, and more savoury than vegetable, it's the ideal base for most ingredients. I don't think you need the red wine or tinned tomatoes that Mr Oliver puts into his early autumn minestrone either — they make it too rich and tomatoey, overpowering the vegetables which should be the real stars of the show.

A good tip from Locatelli is to add the ingredients in the order they will cook, rather than sticking everything in together and hoping for the best. This way you should end up with soft, rather than mushy veg — and not a lump of soup powder in sight.

Serves 4

3 tablespoons olive oil, plus extra to serve
1 onion, chopped
1 clove of garlic, crushed
2 carrots, cut into 1cm dice
2 sticks of celery, cut into 1cm dice
Seasonal vegetables (e.g. autumn/winter — ¼ of a Savoy cabbage, roughly chopped, 1 bunch of spinach, roughly chopped, 1 leek, chopped; spring/summer — 1 courgette, diced, handful of fresh peas or broad beans, ½ a head of fennel, diced)
1.25 litres good-quality chicken stock (see page 173)
1 potato, peeled and cut into 2cm dice
100g drained tinned borlotti beans
200g risotto rice (optional)

Salt and pepper
A small bunch of basil, to serve
50g Parmesan, grated, to serve

1. Heat the olive oil in a heavy-based saucepan over a fairly gentle heat. Add the onion and garlic, cover and cook for 5 minutes, until softened but not coloured. Add the carrots and cook for a few minutes until softened, then do the same with the celery. Add the rest of the vegetables in order of cooking time – spinach or peas cook very quickly, for example, while a cabbage will take longer. (Bear in mind they don't need to be cooked through at this point, just softened.)
2. Pour in the stock, and add the potato, beans and rice, if using. Bring to the boil, then turn down the heat and simmer until the potato and rice are cooked. Season to taste. Serve with torn basil leaves, a scattering of Parmesan and a drizzle of olive oil.

Perfect
Ratatouille

A stalwart of the 1980s dinner party, ratatouille always gave the impression of being an ancient peasant dish one might have picked up from some darling ancient peasant neighbours of Peter Mayle, when in fact, according to Alan Davidson's wonderful *Oxford Companion to Food*, it's a relatively recent creation. The word, which comes from the French *touiller*, to stir, first pops up in 1877, misspelled, in reference to a meat stew. It is not until the 1930s that it becomes associated with a 'ragoût of aubergine with tomatoes, courgettes and sweet pepper'. So authenticity probably isn't something we need to worry about with ratatouille, which is fortunate, given the variety of recipes out there.

A ragoût, of course, suggests something cooked long and slow on the hob – but there is some debate about whether the constituent parts should be cooked together, or separately. Raymond Blanc simmers everything together until tender, which gives a sort of vegetable stew – nice enough, but no more than the sum of its parts. Gui Gedda and Marie-Pierre Moine's *Cooking School Provence* (which promises to teach me to 'shop, cook and eat like a native') demands I char and skin the peppers, blanch and skin the tomatoes, and employ two pans to cook everything separately before combining it into one creamy, but oddly thin stew. Nigel Slater takes the same approach, but sticks the cooked vegetables into the oven instead of simmering them on the hob – which leaves the ratatouille tasty but dry.

In fact, it's a cartoon rat who delivers my ratatouille breakthrough — when making their 2007 film of the same name, the Pixar animation team turned to American chef Thomas Keller, the first American chef to preside over two three-Michelin-starred establishments (New York's Per Se and California's legendary French Laundry), for advice on creating a realistic restaurant kitchen. It's his version of the titular recipe which allows the fictional rat to win over France's toughest restaurant reviewer, and although time-consuming to prepare, it's surprisingly simple: thinly sliced vegetables slow-baked in a pepper, tomato and onion sauce. Although my efforts are not quite as beautiful as the rodent's, I can see why this dish wowed the cartoon critic: the slightly caramelized vegetables on top are earthily sweet, and those beneath meltingly tender from their long, slow steaming, while the sauce is deep and rich, and jammy rather than watery. Much as I hate to admit it, this is one peasant dish which really benefits from tarting up.

Faffing about with Keller's kaleidoscopic vegetable spirals and delicately drizzled vinaigrettes is a step too far for most of us, however: my ratatouille is more homely in style, with slightly chunkier vegetables tossed together on a base of *piperade* with a splash of balsamic vinegar and a pinch of saffron (the last stolen from Joël Robuchon, French restaurant guide Gault Millau's chef of the century — it may have been the last century, but the tip still holds good today). It tastes just as good as the fancy version, and has the benefit of being much quicker to assemble — you can chop the vegetables as the sauce is reducing, chuck it all into the dish, then sit back and enjoy a glass or two of rosé while it's cooking, which seems much more in the spirit of things. It goes without saying that this is a summer dish; you need ripe Mediterranean vegetables for it to work.

Serves 4

2 red peppers
2 tablespoons olive oil, plus
    extra for oiling the tray
1 medium onion, finely diced
4 cloves of garlic, minced
4 ripe tomatoes, peeled, deseeded (page 144)
    and cut into small dice, plus juices
3 sprigs of thyme, plus 1 teaspoon thyme leaves
A pinch of saffron
Salt and pepper
1 teaspoon balsamic vinegar
3 courgettes (a mix of yellow and green
    is good if possible), thinly sliced
1 aubergine, thinly sliced
4 plum tomatoes, thinly sliced
1 tablespoon extra virgin olive oil,
    plus extra to serve

1. Preheat the oven to 230°C/450°F/gas 8. Cut the peppers in half, removing the seeds and pith, and place them cut-side down on a lightly oiled baking tray. Roast for 20 minutes, until the skin has blistered, then remove and leave to cool, turning the oven down to 140°C/275°F/gas 1.

2. Meanwhile, heat the olive oil over a low heat. Add the onion and cook until very soft, but not browned (about 8 minutes), adding three-quarters of the minced garlic 5 minutes in. Stir in the tomatoes and juices, and the sprigs of thyme, and simmer until most of the liquid has evaporated.

3. Peel the peppers, cut into small dice and add to the pan with

the saffron. Cook gently for 5 minutes, then remove the thyme
sprigs and discard, season to taste, and stir in the vinegar.

4. Spread the sauce on the bottom of an ovenproof dish, and arrange
the sliced vegetables on top. Mix the remaining garlic with the
extra virgin olive oil and thyme leaves, season and sprinkle over
the top. Cover tightly with foil, and put into the oven for 2 hours,
until the vegetables are tender to the point of a knife.

5. Remove the foil, and cook for 30 minutes more – if the top
starts to brown, cover loosely with the foil again. If there is any
liquid left in the dish after cooking, decant it into a small pan,
reduce over a medium heat, then stir back in. At this point the
dish can be kept for a couple of days.

6. Just before serving, reheat if desired, then put the ratatouille
under a hot grill until lightly browned. Serve with extra virgin
olive oil and crusty bread.

- -

To salt, or not to salt
Once upon a time, every recipe involving the
magnificent glossy aubergine began with the same
instruction – salt to draw out the bitter juices, then
rinse and pat dry. Such unpalatable flavours have
largely been bred out of the modern aubergine,
but salting still has its adherents, including Delia
Smith, who believes it concentrates the flavour, Hugh
Fearnley-Whittingstall, who thinks it stops them
soaking up quite so much oil, and Skye Gyngell, who
doesn't trouble to explain her reasoning. In fact, as far
as I can tell, all it does is make the aubergine taste salty
– there's no appreciable difference in texture at all.

Fungi's Dirty Little Secret
Everyone from Gordon Ramsay
to the British Mushroom Bureau
urges you not to wash your
mushrooms before cooking —
fungi absorb water like nobody's
business, they say, and who wants to eat a sponge?
Following a series of rigorous tests, however, food
writer Harold McGee has concluded that soaking
mushrooms for prolonged periods makes so little
difference to their water content that we can spritz
our shiitake and bathe our buttons with a clear
conscience.

How to cook vegetables
Many vegetables need nothing more than a quick
peep at boiling water to turn them into the perfect
foil for a rich, creamy fish pie, or a meaty stew. All
the below should be seasoned and
tossed with a knob of butter, or a
dash of olive oil, before serving, and,
if you're making a real effort, some
chopped herbs. In fact, take that as
a general rule: a sprinkle of green
stuff (or lemon zest or toasted
nuts) is the culinary equivalent of
dressing to impress.

Broccoli: Wash and cut into evenly-sized florets, and chop the stalk into batons. Put into a steamer, and cook for about 10 minutes, until tender. The leaves that surround sprouting broccoli stems are perfectly edible, and should be left on unless they're particularly large and tough-looking (leave the stem whole, and serve, like asparagus, with hollandaise or a soft-boiled egg). All broccoli has a particular affinity with anchovies, chilli flakes, lemon zest and garlic.

Cabbage, kale and other leaves: Wash and cut into strips, discarding the woody central core of each cabbage leaf, and put into a steaming basket or colander set over a pan of simmering water. Steam for 4–6 minutes, depending on the vegetable, until soft, but not mushy. All these work extremely well with bacon, chilli and garlic, and chestnuts are also a seasonal possibility.

Carrots: Wash and peel, if necessary (young carrots will not need this), cut into rounds or batons, and steam for about 10 minutes until tender. Carrots can be dressed up with orange zest and hazelnuts, or fresh ginger, chives or parsley, and are even more interesting roasted until soft and caramelized with olive oil and cumin seeds.

Peas and beans: Top and tail runner beans and cut into diagonal pieces if you're feeling fancy, pod peas and broad beans if necessary and peel the beans if they are large – early in the summer season, the skins will be tender enough to eat. Put into a pan of boiling salted water and cook for

2 (peas) to 4 minutes (peas and beans) depending
on their size. As well as the classic fresh mint, peas
and beans pair brilliantly with bacon, smoked fish
and aniseedy tarragon.

Spinach and chard: The big leaves have a better
flavour than the baby salad ones, if you can find
them. Wash well, picking out any grit, then
pat dry and put into a large pan. Cover and
cook over a low heat until they wilt – the water
clinging to the leaves should be enough to keep
them from sticking to the pan. Turn up the heat
and cook, stirring, until the remaining water
has evaporated. As well as the garlic, anchovies
and lemon zest which work so nicely with the
cabbage family, spinach and chard can be made
considerably less healthy, if even more delicious,
with cream or crème fraîche, cheese and nutmeg –
and Jane Grigson recommends stirring in some
Marmite along with the dairy, which gives it an
'unidentifiable, savoury accent'.

Perfect
Coleslaw

*I*f you've never tried homemade coleslaw, you probably think it's made with salad cream. I've given the matter some thought, and that's the only explanation I can come up with for that oddly sweet, vinegary flavour that most supermarket versions share — and as for the aggressive raw onion that some of them sneak in, well, that can ruin a romantic picnic before either of you have had a chance to spill cider on the rug.

In fact, mayonnaise should be the base for coleslaw as we know it — although, as Nigel Slater points out, it can also be made with vinaigrette, which is particularly nice in summer. Darina Allen's *Ballymaloe Cookery Course* adds a dash of yoghurt, presumably for its tangy flavour, but in practice, a little vinegar is more effective. Simon Hopkinson and Lindsey Bareham macerate the shredded vegetables for an hour in salt, sugar and vinegar before mixing in the mayonnaise, which cuts through the richness of the eggs perfectly.

Despite slicing it ever so thinly in obedience to Darina's instructions, I can't get on with raw onion, but I find the chives get lost in Simon and Lindsey's recipe, so I like to compromise with spring onion. Horseradish, rather than Dijon mustard, gives a touch of spice — the Germanic flavour seems more apt here, somehow.

Serve as a side salad or sneak some into a ham sandwich – trust me, on brown bread, it beats pickle hands down.

Serves 4

2 medium carrots
½ a medium white cabbage
1 teaspoon salt
1 teaspoon caster sugar
1 tablespoon white wine vinegar
5 tablespoons mayonnaise (see page 150)
1 tablespoon creamed horseradish
2 spring onions (optional)

1. Peel the carrots and grate into a large bowl. Quarter the cabbage, cut the hard, woody core out of the centre, then shred finely with a sharp knife and add to the carrots.

2. Sprinkle over the salt, sugar and vinegar, mix well, then tip the vegetables into a colander or sieve and leave to macerate over the sink for about an hour. If you're making your mayonnaise, this is the time to do it.

3. Mix the mayonnaise and the horseradish in the bowl, and taste – add a little more if you prefer it hotter. Finely shred the spring onions, if using.

4. Press down on the vegetables to drain any excess liquid, then tip them back into the bowl and add the spring onions. Toss well until mixed, taste for seasoning and serve immediately: it will keep, but the dressing may begin to separate.

Perfect
Cauliflower Cheese

Ah, cauliflower cheese. Floury sauce, mushy vegetables, stringy cheese – this is one comfort food I'd often rather swap for a salad. It has to be made with care: the top should be slightly crunchy, the cauliflower tender, but not to the point of disintegration, and the sauce agreeably piquant.

Saying that, you can get too fancy – I don't think the dish requires a béchamel base, as specified by Simon Hopkinson and Lindsey Bareham; that sauce's onion and bay leaf flavours just confuse the issue. Neither do I think the cook needs to fuss about with double cream, in fact, better to use a plain white sauce for such a nursery classic. Tom Norrington-Davies has the right idea, co-opting this basic as the vehicle for vast amounts of cheese. Lancashire, as it happens, which gives the dish a pleasant saltiness; Cheddar, as suggested by Nigel Slater, is more strident. Cauliflower cheese is a quiet dish by nature – although a pinch of mustard powder, in homage to the surviving fat lady, Clarissa Dickson-Wright, adds a touch of understated spice to proceedings.

Clarissa also gives instructions for baking an entire cauliflower – which looks majestic, but is, in practice, quite difficult to get right. I'm sticking with florets – topped with Simon and Lindsey's breadcrumbs, which provide that all-important crunch that separates cauliflower cheese from rather dreary invalid food.

Serves 4

50g unsalted butter
25g plain flour
300ml milk
½ teaspoon salt
1 teaspoon English mustard powder
100g Lancashire cheese, grated
1 medium cauliflower, leaves removed, broken into evenly
    sized florets
30g breadcrumbs

1. Preheat the oven to 200°C/400°F/gas 6. Melt the butter in a
   medium pan, and stir in the flour to make a roux. Cook on a
   low heat for a couple of minutes, stirring occasionally, but do
   not allow to colour.
2. Pour a little of the milk into the roux, and whisk to combine,
   then gradually add the rest in the same manner until you have a
   smooth liquid. Cook, stirring regularly, until it has thickened
   enough to coat the back of a wooden spoon. Remove from the
   heat, add the salt, mustard powder and half the cheese, and set
   aside.
3. Meanwhile, cook the cauliflower in a pan of salted, boiling water
   for 3 minutes, until softened, but not cooked through.
4. Drain the cauliflower and tip into a buttered baking dish. Tip
   over the sauce, then mix together the breadcrumbs and the
   rest of the cheese and scatter over the top. Bake for about
   30 minutes, or until golden and bubbling.

Perfect
Baked Beans

I try never to run out of baked beans: like anchovies and dried pasta, a tin of beans is insurance against starvation. I've never eaten a bowl of cereal for dinner, and with beans in the house, I'll never have to.

Although I'm a big fan of Britain's leading brand, I don't think it's heresy to acknowledge that they are not the only bean – the sweet, dark Boston sort spring to mind, as do the Mexican *frijoles de olla*.

 These homemade ones are a thicker, spicier take on the familiar tomato-based sort, however – Gary Rhodes does make a pretty good facsimile of them, using red wine vinegar, passata and bean cooking water, but there doesn't seem much point in going to all that trouble when you can buy the real thing so easily.

Baking the beans and sauce together as in Tana Ramsay's recipe (the wife of Gordon has carved out her own niche as an expert family cook – perhaps fortunately, because he doesn't look the kind of man who's home in time for tea every evening), rather than cooking them separately on the hob as Gary Rhodes does, encourages the flavours to blend together, and the sauce to grow comfortingly thick. The red onion, as used by Angela Boggiano in *delicious* magazine, works with the ketchup and vinegar to re-create the distinctive sweet and sour flavour we're all hooked on, while I like to think the smoked paprika adds a whiff of the campfire to the dish.

I have tried making these with tinned beans, but they weren't quite as flavourful — if you must, however, start from step 2 and replace the cooking water with tap water. Oddly, the beans are much better the next day — which is a good argument for freezing a few batches.

Serves 6

300g dried haricot beans,
    soaked in cold water overnight
1 onion, quartered
1 carrot, quartered
1 stick of celery, quartered
½ a bay leaf
2 tablespoons olive oil
1 small red onion, finely chopped
2 cloves of garlic, crushed
2 tablespoons red wine vinegar
½ teaspoon smoked paprika
A pinch of ground cloves
2 teaspoons light brown sugar
1 tablespoon Worcestershire sauce
1 tablespoon tomato ketchup
300ml tomato passata
Salt and pepper

1. Drain the soaked beans, put into a large pan, add the onion, carrot, celery and bay leaf and cover with cold water. Bring to the boil, then turn down the heat and simmer uncovered for about an hour, until the beans are tender. Drain, reserving the cooking liquid but discarding the vegetables and bay leaf.

2. Preheat the oven to 150°C/300°F/gas 2. Put a flameproof casserole on to a lowish heat and add the oil, red onion and garlic. Cook until softened, then turn up the heat and add the red wine vinegar. Simmer until it has nearly all evaporated, then add the paprika, cloves and brown sugar. Cook, stirring, for a couple of minutes, then add the Worcestershire sauce and ketchup and stir well. Pour in the passata and 200ml of the bean cooking liquid, stir well, season and bring to the boil.

3. Cover the casserole and put into the oven for about 2 hours, until you have a thick sauce. Season to taste. These beans are even better reheated, so it's worth making up a big batch and freezing the rest. Keep any leftover bean liquid — the sauce will thicken as it cools, and you may wish to add some more when reheating.

Beans means . . .
Chefs' suggestions for those beans and pulses lurking at the back of the pantry. All recipes available online.

Gordon Ramsay: Spicy mixed bean stew topped with soured cream and paprika
Hugh Fearnley-Whittingstall: Hearty chickpea, potato and kale curry
Nigella Lawson: Speedy smoked cod and cannellini beans
Jamie Oliver: 'Cool' Mexican bean wraps
Keith Floyd: Chuck wagon pork and beans

CHAPTER 5

Sauces and Accompaniments

As the cornerstone of classical French cuisine, the mere mention of sauces, ketchup aside, can put the fear of God into most plain British cooks. Ever practical, Len Deighton brings them down to earth with a bang: 'a sauce', he announces matter-of-factly, 'is a thickened liquid'. And if you bear that in mind, and remember that gravy's a sauce — and any self-respecting granny can knock that up while listening to *The Archers* and keeping half an eye on the crossword — they become a little less scary.

Even Julia Child, the woman who introduced American home cooks to French cuisine, and who wasn't entirely immune to its grandeur herself, admits there is nothing 'secret or mysterious' about sauces — once you know how to make a few basic 'mother sauces', such as mayonnaise, you're equipped to produce 'the whole towering edifice'. If they didn't have such intimidating names, I reckon we'd all be happily making hollandaise for eggs Benedict every Sunday morning without a second thought.

For the most part, the great sauces of the traditional kitchen —
hollandaise, béarnaise, mayonnaise — require nerve and know-how,
rather than any great skill. If you *know* that an unpromising-looking
bowl of egg yolk and oil will eventually thicken into something that
will knock anything Mr Hellman has to offer into a cocked hat, as
long as you stick at it, then success becomes just a question of
patience — and faith. The problem with sauces as far as I'm
concerned is that once you've tasted a homemade pesto, or
guacamole, the shop-bought kind will never seem quite as good
again. Ignorance is bliss, as they say.

Perfect
Tomato Sauce

*T*omato sauce is one of the cornerstones of the modern kitchen – handy for a thousand things, from quick pasta dishes to curry bases – so it makes sense to find a recipe you like, and make up a big batch to freeze. After all, you can cook all the Heston recipes you like, but if someone opens your fridge to find a jar of overpriced ready-made stuff you're rumbled.

In Italy, spiritual if not ancestral home of the tomato, such sauces are made with both fresh and tinned tomatoes, depending on the season. They're wise enough to realize there's little point in trying to force flavour out of the thin fruits of the winter months – and, unless you have a glut of overripe ones on your hands, I'd be inclined to stick with the tinned sort all year round in this country, and enjoy any truly excellent tomatoes you might come across in a salad instead.

Giorgio Locatelli uses a mixture of fresh and tinned tomatoes in the sauce at his London restaurant, which he says is best in summer – but, probably because his suppliers are better than mine, I find his recipe rather acidic. The River Café's rich tomato sauce calls for Italian peeled plum tomatoes packed in their own juice, slow cooked with onions and garlic, which gives a much fuller flavour – but it's Angela Hartnett's tip about adding a little sugar that makes all the difference. A dash of tomato purée makes the sauce even richer, and flavourful enough to need nothing but a drizzle of olive oil, or a sprinkling of basil leaves, to make a winning pasta dish.

If you prefer your sauce even sweeter, however, consider using a red onion instead, as the River Café does — you shouldn't see the bits, because it will melt into the sauce as it cooks, but it will give a jammier result. I think leaving the herbs until serving makes the finished sauce more versatile, and slightly fresher tasting, but you can add thyme, oregano or even chilli along with the onion if you prefer.

Serves 4

5 tablespoons olive oil
1 small onion, very finely sliced
1 clove of garlic, very finely sliced
A pinch of salt
A pinch of sugar
1 teaspoon tomato purée
2 x 400g tins of Italian plum tomatoes in juice

1. Put the olive oil into a deep heavy-based frying pan over a lowish heat. Add the onion and cook very gently until completely softened, but not browned — this should take at least 10 minutes. Add the garlic and cook for another 5 minutes.
2. Stir in a generous pinch of salt and sugar and the tomato purée, then tip in the plum tomatoes and roughly break up with a wooden spoon. Cook, stirring occasionally, for about 35 minutes, until thick and jammy. Taste, and add a little more sugar or salt if necessary.

How to skin and deseed a tomato
Cut a small cross in the base, then plunge the
tomato into boiling water for 20 seconds. Remove
into a bowl of ice-cold water to cool down – the skin
should then just peel off.

Cut the tomato into quarters, and scoop out the
seeds with a teaspoon – most of the flavour is in the
seeds and the jelly that surrounds them, however, so
do this over a bowl to catch the juices and add these
to whatever you're making along with the flesh.

Never keep tomatoes in the fridge
They don't like the cold, and will become tasteless
and woolly. Keep them at room temperature
instead.

Perfect
Hollandaise

*T*he secret of hollandaise is, I think, confidence. You need to show
this sauce who's boss from the start – no mollycoddling it with a
bain-marie, Mr Slater, or fiddling about with a blender in its
honour, à la Delia Smith. As long as you have a heavy-based
pan, and a modicum of self-respect, you can make it straight in
the pan.

Although hollandaise is one of the classic sauces of the French
kitchen, there is some debate about whether to use clarified or whole
butter to thicken it, and if lemon juice or vinegar is better for
flavouring. Gary Rhodes, Gordon Ramsay and Michel
Roux all come down in the clarified camp, which means
melting the butter and skimming off the milk solids from
the top, to leave just the butterfat, before whisking it into
the sauce. It's not hard to do, but it is fiddly, and I find
that I prefer the flavour of the whole butter, even if the end
result isn't quite so thick. (The solids also contain water, so
leaving them in will give a thinner sauce.)

The great Escoffier used vinegar in his sauce, but I think that takes
this a little bit close to the béarnaise below – lemon keeps things
fresh, and is particularly nice with vegetables, which is, of course,
hollandaise's dream date come summertime.

Serve with grilled fish, steamed asparagus or sprouting broccoli, or, best of all, as the star attraction of eggs Benedict, that heavenly breakfast dish of toasted muffins, poached eggs and ham.

Makes 300ml

4 large free-range egg yolks
1 tablespoon white wine vinegar
250g cold unsalted butter, diced
¼ of a lemon
Salt and pepper

1. Put the yolks, vinegar, butter and 2 tablespoons of water into a pan and heat very gently, whisking all the time. As the butter melts, the sauce will begin to thicken – don't be tempted to hurry things along by turning the heat up; the sides of the saucepan should be cool enough to touch at all points. Do not leave your station at the pan under any circumstances, imminent danger excepted.

2. Once the butter has melted, turn up the heat to medium-low and whisk vigorously until the sauce thickens – if it begins to steam, take it off the heat, but do not stop whisking.

3. When the sauce is thickened to your taste, stir in 1 tablespoon of lemon juice and some seasoning. Taste and adjust if necessary. Serve immediately, or store in a warm place or even a thermos flask until needed – hollandaise does not reheat very well.

—aise doctor

If your hollandaise or béarnaise begins to split, it probably means it's got too hot. Take the pan off the heat and stand it in a bowl of cold water (it's useful to have one of these by the hob just in case), whisking as you go. Add a tablespoon of cold water and whisk vigorously; it should come back.

Any leftovers will solidify in the fridge. Take a tip from *Toronto Star* food editor Susan Sampson and put the hollandaise or béarnaise in a small metal bowl inside a larger bowl. Half fill the outer bowl with hot, but not boiling water, and leave the sauce for 5 minutes before stirring; if you keep doing this, you should eventually be able to coax it back to life. If it curdles, however, follow the advice above.

Perfect
Béarnaise

*T*he difference between these two great sauces, to those unschooled in classical French cookery, is basically one of flavour – while most hollandaises are finished with the barest squeeze of lemon to cut through the butter and egg, béarnaise is much more of a big hitter in the taste stakes, with vinegar, shallots and herbs all putting in an appearance. I've given a more classic method for this sauce – you can also use this for the hollandaise, disregarding the first step, if you run into problems.

Larousse add chervil, and John Burton-Race, the former Michelin-starred chef turned daytime TV star, parsley, but I think all béarnaise needs is a generous amount of tarragon – one of the more underrated herbs, and one that should be allowed to shine here. Serve with steak (see page 54), or any grilled meat or fish.

Makes 300ml

> 2 shallots, finely chopped
> ½ a bay leaf
> A small bunch of tarragon,
>   separated into leaves and stalks
> 4 tablespoons white wine vinegar
> 4 large free-range egg yolks
> 250g cold unsalted butter, diced
> Salt and pepper

1. Put the shallots, bay leaf, tarragon stalks and vinegar into a small pan. Bring to the boil, then simmer until almost all the liquid has evaporated. Take off the heat, add a tablespoon of water, allow to cool slightly, then strain through a fine sieve and discard the solids.

2. Put the egg yolks into a heavy-based pan over a very low heat and whisk in the vinegar reduction. Add the butter piece by piece, adding another as soon as one melts, and whisking well all the time. The sauce will gradually start to thicken.

3. If it becomes too thick, or begins to look like scrambled eggs, take off the heat immediately and add up to 1 tablespoon of cold water, a little at a time. Stir in the finely chopped tarragon leaves and season to taste before serving.

Perfect
Mayonnaise

Shop-bought mayonnaise is one of those things that's so different from its homemade counterpart that, like instant coffee, or oven chips, it ought to come with a warning prefix – whether you like the pale, wobbly mass-produced stuff or not, you have to agree that even the very best (by which I obviously mean the most expensive) versions bear little resemblance to the rich, yellow sauce which slips so silkily over a side of poached salmon in the picnic of your dreams.

The jar I have in front of me, the own-brand of a terribly respectable supermarket, lists ten ingredients, including wheat-glucose-fructose syrup and colouring. Classical mayonnaise requires just three: egg yolks, oil and vinegar, and as Michel Roux points out in the first episode of the excellent late 80s television series *The Roux Brothers* (available online), it's very easy to make at home – although it might take you longer to separate the eggs than it takes them to whip up a batch and some new potatoes to go with it.

Mayonnaise is a simple emulsion of oil in water, egg yolks being half water. As any cookbook will tell you, it's important to dribble in the oil very gradually, or you will overwhelm the yolk, and end up with an egg yolk in oil mixture, rather than the other way around – and this will curdle. The Roux brothers add theirs with cavalier speed, and in theory, according to Harold McGee, the oil can be added in doses of up to a third of the volume of the yolk at a time, but after a few disasters, I decide to stick to Delia's drop-by-drop method. (Her instant mayonnaise, made in a food processor, is, as she observes, runnier than the classic version, but it's streets ahead of anything you can buy. Check it out.)

Add salt at the beginning, to help thicken the yolk, but leave the vinegar to the end – I've tried out Julia Child's recipe from *Mastering the Art of French Cooking*, which begins with the acid, but this seems to give a thinner result. I have picked up one useful tip from the 'American Elizabeth David', however: beating the yolks 'until thick and sticky' before adding the oil. This makes them, according to Child, 'ready to receive the oil' – which makes sense if, as McGee suggests, the more solid the yolks, the easier they are to mix with the oil.

Now we've established the method, it's time to turn to ingredients. There's a tendency these days to assume that olive oil, with its healthy reputation and biblical heritage, is always the best choice, and it has its devotees in Elizabeth David and Theo Randall, but I notice that Michel Roux suggests using groundnut oil instead, although, he says, you can add a little extra virgin olive oil at the end if you like, just for flavour. I have tried an all-olive mayonnaise with an oil which declared itself to be light, but found the flavour harsh and overpowering. Add a dash or two of your favourite extra virgin at the end instead if you want that peculiarly green flavour.

Michel Roux also suggests two different acids: warm wine vinegar, or cold lemon juice. McGee debunks the idea that the temperature of any liquid you add at the end will make a difference to its texture, but it will, he says, help thin the mixture, as well as, in the case of the acids, helping to stabilize it. Whether you, like Michel, like lemon juice, or side with Albert and his vinegar, is up to you, just as the kind of mustard you put in (I use Dijon), and whether you want to add garlic, is a matter for personal preference: I think lemon goes better with olive oil and with fish, whereas the vinegar matches well with salads.

Really, however, once you've achieved the sacred mayonnaise, you can add whatever you like: grapefruit, truffles – even soy sauce, although please not when I'm coming to dinner. Or, of course, you can just sit there and stare in wonderment at the amazing thing you've created.

Makes 300ml

> 2 large free-range egg yolks
> A generous pinch of salt
> 250ml groundnut or sunflower oil
> 25ml extra virgin olive, walnut or rapeseed oil
> I teaspoon white wine vinegar or lemon juice
> I teaspoon mustard of your choice (or I teaspoon mustard powder)

1. Make sure all the ingredients are at room temperature before starting. Place a damp tea towel beneath a large mixing bowl, and add the egg yolks. Beat well with an electric whisk for a minute or so – you can do it by hand with a balloon whisk, but bear in mind it will take a lot longer.
2. Add the salt and continue to beat well for 30 seconds, until the yolk is thick and sticky. Begin to add the neutral oil, a tablespoon at a time, beating all the while, and making sure each

is incorporated before adding the next — don't be tempted to rush this, or your mayonnaise will split. You can begin to add the oil in slightly larger amounts once you've mixed in about half. If the mayonnaise becomes too thick, and hard to beat, add 1 tablespoon of warm water to the mixture and whisk it in before adding any more oil.

3. Once you've incorporated all the neutral oil, switch to the olive oil and add it in the same way. Once it is all incorporated, beat the mayonnaise for another 30 seconds until thick and glossy, then add the vinegar or lemon juice, and the mustard, and mix in.

4. Stir in any further ingredients, such as chopped herbs or anchovy essence, then cover and keep refrigerated until you are ready to eat.

- -

Marvellous mayonnaise
Crushed garlic may be the most obvious tweak that springs to mind here (aïoli is delicious with fish, cold chicken and crudités), but mayonnaise is a master of reinvention.

Anchovy mayonnaise: Puréed anchovies (serve with vegetable fritters — it goes particularly well with cauliflower — fried mushrooms or calamari)
Dijonnaise: Dijon mustard (cold meats, particularly pork)
Rémoulade: Dijon mustard, garlic and pepper (folded through shredded raw celeriac or carrot to make a classic French salad)
Tartare: Chopped gherkins, capers, tarragon

and parsley (usually served with fried foods, particularly fish; it would be ideal with the fishcakes on page 71)

Watercress: Finely chopped watercress (cold fish, especially poached salmon)

Perfect
Vinaigrette

On a recent trip to Paris, I was reminded of why, for all their fondness for le Big Mac and enormous hypermarkets, the French can still teach us a thing or two about good food. My epiphany came in the form of a side salad, a simple dish of lamb's lettuce – no micro herbs, or heirloom radishes – dressed with the most perfect of vinaigrettes. It clung lightly to every tiny leaf, a delicate essay in culinary restraint – the kick of the vinegar, the heat of the mustard, the seasoning – all finely balanced so as to complement, but not overpower, the dish.

In his *Bouchon* cookbook, the Californian chef Thomas Keller prefaces a recipe for vinaigrette with the arresting thought that it might even be 'the perfect sauce'. Hang on a minute, you might think – it's up against some pretty stiff competition. But whereas a béchamel, or a velouté, repel creative customization, the good-natured vinaigrette positively encourages it. Plus, it can be put together in under five minutes, which is not something you can say for anything involving a roux.

As the vinaigrette, or *sauce ravigote*, also goes by the name 'French dressing' (although, like the unappetizing-sounding 'French stick', this seems to have fallen from favour in recent years), it makes sense to consult the original Gallic cookery Bible, *Larousse Gastronomique*, for a definitive recipe.

'Dissolve a little salt in 1 tablespoon vinegar,' it counsels. 'Add 3 tablespoons oil and some pepper.' That's it – unless you want to get creative with mustard and the like. But it's this basic recipe which interests me. A 3:1 ratio of oil and vinegar seems a good one – 2:1, which I have seen elsewhere as 'sacred for the best and thickest vinaigrette', is too thin and acidic, and any more oil is difficult to incorporate properly.

I like the vegetable oil suggested by *Larousse*; I used to use extra virgin olive oil, but their vinaigrette has a much lighter, silkier feel, and tastes fresher without the slightly overpowering flavour of extra virgin. It also seems to mix more easily, and takes longer to separate. But it seems a shame to use such a bland oil in one of the few recipes in which the stuff really shines, so I suggest a compromise: a 2:1 vegetable/extra virgin olive oil mix, which combines a light texture with just a hint of peppery greenness.

Vinaigrette is what is known in the trade as an unstable emulsion – two liquids (water, in the form of vinegar, and oil) that, in the words of the great Harold McGee, 'can't mix evenly with each other', and which will eventually separate back into their original forms. You can slow this process down by adding an emulsifier, which will act as a bond between the two ingredients. Many commercial dressings use a fatty substance called lecithin, but at home it's much easier, and tastier, to add a flavouring that will do the same job.

Although wisdom has it that you can use everything from egg yolk (which, in my opinion, starts to stray dangerously into mayonnaise territory) to cold mashed potato to stabilize your dressing, the most popular choices are things which actively complement the existing ingredients – miso paste, for a Japanese-style vinaigrette with rice vinegar, for example, or tahini if you're feeling a bit Middle Eastern. For a more classic flavour, I generally use mustard – because it's already emulsified, ready-made mustard gives a thicker, more mustardy finish than powder.

Whisked into a vinaigrette at the end, mustard adds heat, but has very little effect on how long the dressing holds together. Stir it into the vinegar along with the salt before you add the oil, however, and your sauce should be good for quarter of an hour or so. Honey rounds out the flavour nicely.

Although a whisk makes a perfectly decent dressing, if I'm making large amounts I take a tip from Thomas Keller and use a blender to start my vinaigrette off – if you do it all in there, it will become unpalatably gloopy. The blender smashes the oil and water molecules up so finely that it takes them ages to reassemble and subsequently separate, and it lasts days in the fridge. Normally, however, you can't beat a simple jar – very little washing up, and after all, a dressing only needs to stay together for as long as it takes you to eat the salad.

So, as long as you stick to the ratio of oil and vinegar that suits your taste (different vinegars, in particular, vary in strength, so be careful with anything new), and keep a balance of flavours in mind, the world's best sauce is now your playground. Why, I've even heard rumours of a bacon fat version . . .

A pinch of salt
A generous ½ teaspoon Dijon mustard
A generous ½ teaspoon honey
1 tablespoon red wine vinegar
2 tablespoons vegetable oil
1 tablespoon extra virgin olive oil

1. Put the salt, mustard and honey into a jar, and mix together into a paste. Add the vinegar, and stir well to combine.
2. Pour in the oils, screw the lid on tightly, and shake until you have an emulsion. Store in the fridge.

How to dress a salad
First, make sure your leaves are completely dry, or they'll repel the dressing. Second, I find it helpful to pour some of the vinaigrette into the base of the serving bowl before adding the salad, and then toss it through the leaves — it seems to give more even coverage. And third, don't dress a green salad until you're ready to eat it — the oil in the dressing will make your leaves look all sad and wilted.

Perfect
Guacamole

Guacamole and I did not get off to a good start. We first met in the context of a home-assembly fajita kit — marinated chicken in a little cellophane pouch, sachets of soured cream and salsa, a few desiccated tortillas and something distinctly unappetizing-looking in a small plastic pot. In those innocent pre-pesto and wasabi days, green food was a bit of a novelty outside the salad aisle, and the colour unnerved me until I realized the contents were, in reality, little more than double cream with a soupçon of avocado paying lip service to the original recipe. How sophisticated I felt, rolling my own dinner.

Now, this was 1994. Leggings and Take That were hot stuff. What puzzles me is why, nearly twenty years later, when both these things have fallen from grace at least twice, the same awful guacamole is still in fashion. It's not as if Mexican food is a novelty; why, these days you can even find restaurants that manage to make money without the help of a hat-stand of amusing headgear and fifteen types of tequila slammer. But somehow the pea green sludge, heavy with dairy and low on flavour, still lurks alongside the hummous and the taramasalata in the chilled aisle.

As I discovered some years later, guacamole should be zingy with lime, to cut through the creamy richness of the ripe avocado. Rick Bayless, one of the finest Mexican chefs north of the Rio Grande, and an award-winning writer on the subject, describes it in his *Mexican Kitchen* cookbook as 'a verdant, thick-textured bowl of festivity, ripe with the elusive flavour of avocado. Mash in a little lime, raw onion, coriander, chilli, perhaps tomato, and the avocado comes fully alive.' I have tried a version with soured cream, but find it bland and heavy.

According to *Bon Appetit* magazine, down Mexico way, 'some cooks coarsely mash avocados, season them with salt – maybe a little garlic – and call the result "guacamole"'. Their point, I think, is that there is no definitive recipe, which means you don't have to worry too much about 'authenticity' – although, after experimentation, I can confirm there is no room for *Bon Appetit*'s aggressive garlic or Bayless' acrid onion in my guacamole; spring onion is about as far as I'm prepared to go down that road.

I'm surprised to discover that Thomasina Miers, founder of Mexican chain Wahaca, doesn't include tomato in the perfect guacamole recipe she supplied to *The Times*, although I notice they do feature in the stuff served in her restaurants. Thank goodness for that, because for me they're a must: the sauce seems sadly one-dimensional without their acidic fruitiness. Bayless made a version of his house guacamole with sun-dried tomatoes for an Obama victory party (Michelle was apparently a big fan of his Chicago restaurant, Topolobampo, before she took off for DC); I prefer to use fresh ones if possible, but it's a good substitute to bear in mind for winter months, when our tomatoes will be watery and thin on flavour. Fresh chillies are also a must for a really sharp guacamole, although smoky chipotles are an interesting variation, particularly if you're serving it with meat, and in an avocado-based emergency, I have used chilli flakes with no ill effect. Aromatic coriander and zingy lime are also non-negotiable: they bring out the flavour of all the other ingredients. If you don't like coriander, I will grudgingly accept flat-leaf parsley as a substitute, but it won't be quite as aromatic.

Guacamole should be made by hand, rather than in a machine – you're not aiming for a purée, but a chunky, creamy salsa. A pestle and mortar is good, but if you don't have one of those big Mexican sort hewn from volcanic rock, a large bowl and a fork or potato masher will do just as well. And, lastly, forget anything you've read about avocado stones keeping it greener for longer – lime juice helps, but the only way to stop avocados turning brown is to keep them away from air, which means pressing clingfilm into the surface until you're ready to serve.

Guacamole is one of those dishes which is happy to be played around with according to taste. The only golden rule is – use ripe avocados!

Makes 500g

1–3 fresh green chillies, depending
 on heat and your taste (1 will give
 a very mild result, 3 an extremely
 spicy one), finely chopped
2 spring onions, thinly sliced
A handful of fresh coriander, roughly chopped
Sea salt
3 ripe avocados (Hass, the knobbly
 brown ones, tend to be the creamiest
 and most flavoursome)
1 ripe medium tomato, cut into 3cm dice
Juice of 1 lime

1. Put a teaspoon each of the chilli, onion and coriander into a pestle and mortar, along with a pinch of sea salt, and grind to a paste.
2. Cut the avocados in half and remove the stones with a teaspoon.

Scoop out the insides, cut into rough cubes, then put into a serving bowl and mash to a chunky paste, leaving some pieces intact.

3. Stir the chilli paste into the avocado, then gently fold in the tomatoes and the rest of the onions, chilli and coriander. Add lime juice and salt to taste. Serve immediately, or cover the surface with clingfilm and refrigerate.

Rolling citrus fruit firmly along the kitchen counter before cutting them open and squeezing them helps to release the juice and makes the job much quicker – if you don't have a citrus reaming tool to help with juicing, use a fork to squeeze the juice out. If a recipe calls for zest as well, always do this before cutting them in half, as it's far easier to zest whole fruit.

The searing truth
Recipes will often urge you to deseed a chilli for a milder result – this isn't, as many people suppose, because the seeds themselves are particularly hot, but because the innocuous white membrane that attaches them to the fruit contains a capsaicin hit hefty enough to blow your head off. Try the pith of a Scotch bonnet and weep – literally. Good ways to soothe the pain include milk, yoghurt, plain rice and bread. Contrary to popular belief, however, mockery does not help one little bit.

Perfect
Pesto

*F*rom sophisticated Italian saucepot to 'middle-class ketchup' in a single generation, pesto has suffered more than most foodstuffs at the hands of the British mania for gastronomic appropriation. In the greedy heat of passion, we've spawned pesto crisps, pesto hummous (shudder) and even pesto oatcakes, but oddly enough, we eat very little of what might be described as 'proper pesto'. The long-life stuff is undoubtedly a useful thing to have in the cupboard for emergencies, but don't kid yourself that it's the authentic taste of the Cinque Terra.

To clarify, we're talking classic pesto, of the kind that was being made in north-west Italy and south-east France long before the Romans and their fermented fish sauce – not 'Japanese pesto', or sun-dried tomato pesto, or anything involving rocket. The backbone of this is, of course, basil: Giorgio Locatelli recommends the smaller, sweeter leaves for the fullest flavour and smoothest texture, but then he also has these leaves flown over specially from Prà, the epicentre of Ligurian pesto production, so he's what might be described as a details man. As long as the herb is fresh, and vibrant in colour, you'll probably be OK.

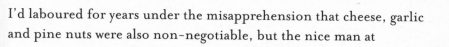

I'd laboured for years under the misapprehension that cheese, garlic and pine nuts were also non-negotiable, but the nice man at

Borough Market set me straight when I went to buy my cheese recently. 'Every pesto is personal,' he told me. 'As long as it has basil, cheese and olive oil, it is pesto.' So, after experimentation, I discover that my particular pesto lacks garlic, like the one in *The Silver Spoon* (raw garlic is a bully – without it, the basil and pine nuts shine all the brighter), and also takes its cue from that book for its cheese, using a mix of fresh, lactic pecorino, and salty, savoury Parmesan. Locatelli just uses pecorino, but I find its more delicate flavour gets lost. Pine nuts are vital for thickening the sauce, and toasting them, as the great chef suggests, really helps to bring out their sweetly nutty flavour.

Even Locatelli admits that if you have to make large quantities of pesto, it's easier to use a food processor, as Marcus Wareing does, but I find that smashing up the basil seems to affect the flavour; a theory confirmed by Harold McGee, who has concluded after experimentation that the larger the pieces of leaf, the slower they are to discolour. Making it in a pestle and mortar may seem time-consuming, but the results speak for themselves – just try and imagine you're on a sun-dappled terrace on the Ligurian coast, rather than in your kitchen, and the minutes will fly by.

Pesto, as we've discovered, is a very amenable condiment, but the traditional way to serve it in Italy is with linguine, green beans and potatoes. Add a little of the pasta cooking water to the pesto to thin it before tossing them together, so it coats the strands better.

Makes 200g

2 tablespoons pine nuts
A pinch of salt
125g fresh basil leaves (pick off as
    much of the stalk as you can, as this
    discolours faster than the leaves)
15g Parmesan, grated
15g pecorino, grated
125ml extra virgin olive oil

1. Toast the pine nuts in a dry pan on a moderate heat, stirring regularly and being careful not to let them burn, and then allow to cool completely. Lightly crush in a pestle and mortar, along with a pinch of salt.
2. Add the basil leaves a few at a time, and, working as quickly as possible, pound them into the mixture until you have a thickish paste.
3. Work in the cheese, then gradually incorporate the oil, reserving a little for the top.
4. Spoon the pesto into a jar, and cover the top with oil. Refrigerate until use.

Perfect
Gravy

*T*here's no French translation for gravy. Their nearest equivalents don't really cut the mustard — you can hardly imagine an effete *jus* powering any sort of train, or everything coming up all *sauce brune*. In Britain, gravy is more than just a condiment; it's liquid comfort. Think of the warm, meaty embrace of every-mother Lynda Bellingham in the Oxo adverts of yesteryear, or that self-satisfied 'ahh, Bisto' slogan which perfectly encapsulated a nation's feelings about a piping jug of gravy — even if we've since realized that making your own is just as easy.

It brings together a Sunday roast like a cup of tea brings together a group of strangers — bestowing a soothing, savoury homeliness on  everything it touches. And, like many traditional favourites, every cook has their own method. As Hugh Fearnley-Whittingstall wisely points out in his *River Cottage Meat Book*, 'there is no recipe for gravy, nor should there be'. There are, however, various ways to make sure you do your patriotic duty by the scrapings in the pan.

First of all, I firmly believe that gravy should be thick — perhaps not quite thick enough to stand a spoon up in, but certainly more robust than a *jus*. For this, you need a roux, and the easiest way to do this is to tip the juices out, make it in the pan with all the lovely crusty bits, then whisk the juices back in. Far quicker than doing it the other way round, and you're much less likely to end up with lumpy gravy.

Michel Roux Jr may know a thing or two about French food, but I am less than convinced by his suggestion about mashing tin-roasted vegetables into the gravy — mushy carrots don't taste any better in liquid form, so if you're going to use what Jamie Oliver describes as a 'vegetable trivet', discard it before you begin making the gravy. I'm equally sceptical about the Royal Society of Chemists' conclusions regarding cabbage cooking water during their investigation into the chemistry of the perfect gravy — ugh. I like a nice Savoy as much as the next person, but it's not a flavour I want to find in a sauce.

More surprisingly, wine isn't an altogether welcome presence either, which is a revelation — most of us add it out of habit, but once you've tried it without, it can't be denied that this makes it taste more like a red wine sauce than an honest British condiment. Perhaps John Torode is right: wine's for drinking with a roast, not for tipping into it. The scientists also suggest adding dark soy sauce to bring out the umami flavours of the meat. Now, I'm happy to add Bovril or Marmite to meat dishes when required, but tipping in such a distinctively Oriental ingredient goes against the grain — particularly when you can taste it in the finished gravy. If your gravy isn't quite up to scratch, I'd recommend using one of these, or a little stock instead — or even umami paste, if you can find it in your local specialist grocers. Alternatively, if you use homemade stock instead of water, you're unlikely to have the problem in the first place. But that's why they're chemists, and not cooks.

Hugh Fearnley-Whittingstall provides a long list of sweeteners, seasonings and aromatizers for gravy, but one he doesn't mention is

English mustard, which is my favoured choice for beef. Mix a teaspoon in at the end and you've got all your sauces in one boat – and the same goes for horseradish. This recipe can be used for other meats, so adjust the condiment as desired; redcurrant jelly for lamb, apple juice for pork, etc.

For perfect gravy, you need good-quality meat, good-quality stock – and that's it. It really is as easy as (meat) pie.

1 tablespoon plain flour
600ml hot good-quality stock,
   preferably homemade (see page 169)
Salt and pepper
Flavourings of your choice (see above)

1. Make the gravy in a flameproof roasting tin while the joint is resting elsewhere. Pour off most of the fat (you can put it through a gravy separating jug if you like), leaving about a tablespoon, as well as the meat juices, and put the tin over a medium heat. Sprinkle over the flour and stir into the fat, scraping to loosen any bits on the bottom of the tin. Cook, stirring, for a couple of minutes, until the flour is slightly browned, being careful not to burn it.
2. Add a ladle of stock to the tin and stir to incorporate. Add the rest of the stock and bring to the boil, stirring. Simmer, stirring regularly, until the gravy has reached your preferred thickness, then season to taste. If you want to add any other flavourings, do so now, then heat through to serve.

Perfect
Stock

*L*ife might seem too short to make your own stock, until you realize that it saves you a fair amount of washing up after the Sunday roast – temporarily at least. Chuck in the bones, the vegetable trimmings and a few elderly herbs, cover with cold water, do a bit of skimming, then sit back in front of a film while time works its traditional magic. Even if you don't have a roast handy, most butchers will give you bones for free, which means you can make one of the cornerstones of culinary greatness for practically nothing. (Although they tend to be over-salted, stock cubes are fine for many things, but when stock plays a pivotal role in a dish, such as a soup or a risotto, you need to step things up a notch.)

There are a few rules to bear in mind when it comes to stock:

- Raw bones will give a clearer stock than cooked ones, but home cooks are unlikely to be unduly troubled by a cloudy stock. Ask your butcher to chop them up to make them easier to fit into your stockpot.
- Stocks made from poultry or vegetables are known as white stocks, and are simply made by simmering bones and aromatics together to extract the flavour. For richer beef, lamb or veal stocks, known as brown stocks, the bones and vegetables are roasted before simmering.

- Adding veal bones or a pig's trotter to any stock will add collagen to the stock, which will help it set to a jelly. This will keep longer than a liquid stock.

- You need more than just bones — I find it helpful to do as Hugh Fearnley-Whittingstall does and think of it as a broth in its own right, rather than just a raw ingredient: that way, it's easier to work out how to make it taste good.

- A good way to do this is using vegetables: carrot, onion, celery and herbs will all add pleasing flavours and aromas to the finished stock; although they can be tops or bottoms, or slightly past their best, never put anything rotten in a stock, because if it didn't taste good to begin with, you can bet your boots it will be even worse when boiled down to a concentrate. There's no need to peel vegetables, as long as they're clean, and extra peelings and tops are also good — herb stalks are ideal. Vegetables to avoid in any quantity are anything starchy (potatoes, yams, etc.), which will make your stock murky, beetroot, which will make it gruesomely pink, and the cabbage family, including broccoli and cauliflower, which will leave it tasting of overcooked sprouts.

- You must start a stock with cold water: hot, according to *Leiths Meat Bible*, will melt the fat in the bones into the stock, making it greasy and unpleasant tasting. With cold, the fat will rise to the surface, where you can skim it off; do this frequently.

- Don't add salt to your stock — it's easier to add salt to the finished dish than it is to correct an over-salted one, and remember, all that reducing will concentrate the flavours.

- Don't boil the stock; keep it at a gentle simmer, so the surface just trembles, or it will be cloudy.

- Don't make the mistake of thinking that the longer you cook your stock, the better it will be – as I've found to my cost, after a while, the flavours turn murky.

- All the recipes below can be scaled up, so you may wish to freeze your ingredients until you have enough to make a really big batch – stock keeps in the fridge for a few days, and freezes well.

The below are basic stocks – for more information, see *Leiths Meat Bible*, which covers the subject very thoroughly.

Vegetable stock

50g butter
2 onions, roughly chopped
2 large carrots, roughly chopped
2 sticks of celery, roughly chopped
Vegetable trimmings of your
    choice, apart from those listed
    above (e.g. leeks, mushrooms,
    fennel, turnips, lettuce,
    beans, etc.)
I bay leaf
A few parsley stalks
A few black peppercorns

1. Melt the butter in a large pan, and stir in the vegetables. Cover the pan and cook over a low heat for about 10 minutes, then add the herbs and peppercorns, cover with water and bring to the boil.
2. Reduce to a simmer and cook for 20 minutes. Pass through a sieve and it's ready to use.

Meat stock

1kg beef or lamb bones
2 onions, quartered
2 carrots, quartered
2 sticks of celery, quartered
100g button mushrooms
1 tablespoon tomato purée
A handful of parsley and/or thyme stalks
1 bay leaf
A few peppercorns

1. Preheat the oven to 220°C/425°F/gas 7. If the bones have any large chunks of fat visible, trim them off, then rinse the bones well under cold water and put them into a large roasting tin with the onions, carrots and celery. Roast, turning occasionally, for an hour, until the bones are well browned. Make sure the vegetables don't burn, as this will spoil the flavour of the finished stock.

2. Using tongs, carefully transfer the hot bones and vegetables into a stockpot, but drain off any fat. Add the rest of the ingredients, including any other vegetables you're using.

3. Pour about 300ml of water into the roasting tin and put it on a medium heat. Bring to the boil and deglaze by scraping up all the caramelized bits from the bottom, then tip this into the stockpot. Cover the bones with cold water, and bring to the boil.

4. Skim off any scum from the surface – you can add a little cold water to help solidify it – then simmer gently (so the surface just trembles, rather than bubbles), uncovered, for 5 hours, skimming from time to time.

5. Strain the stock through a sieve and discard the vegetables – don't press them, as this will make your stock murky.

6. Bring the stock to your required strength by boiling rapidly until reduced; you'll be able to tell how strong it is by tasting it. A useful way to store stock is to boil it until thick and syrupy (a *glace de viande*) — it will keep in the fridge for several weeks like this, and you just need to add water to bring it back to a stock consistency.

Chicken stock

1 chicken carcass (raw or cooked), plus any giblets but not the liver, which will make the stock bitter
1 small onion, roughly chopped
1 carrot, roughly chopped
1 stick of celery, roughly chopped
A few parsley and/or thyme stalks
½ bay leaf
A few peppercorns

1. Put all the ingredients into a large pan and cover with cold water. Bring to the boil and skim off any scum from the top — you can add some cold water to solidify the fat and make this easier.
2. Turn down the heat and simmer for around 4 hours, skimming occasionally, then pass through a sieve, and allow to cool.
3. If you aren't using the stock immediately, you can leave the fat which will solidify on top as a handy natural seal — otherwise, lift it off before adding to your chosen dish. You can also reduce the stock to give a more intense flavour if required. If you're not using it immediately, reduce the stock by boiling it until thick and syrupy (a *glace de viande*) — it will keep in the fridge for several weeks like this, and you just need to add water to bring it back to a stock consistency.

Fish stock

**1kg fish bones, fish heads or prawn,
crab or mussel shells (best to avoid
oily fish or strong-flavoured fish,
though, such as mackerel or salmon,
as they can impart a rancid flavour)
3 leeks, roughly chopped
1 fennel bulb, roughly chopped
2 sticks of celery, roughly chopped
3 carrots, roughly chopped
A handful of parsley stalks
A few peppercorns**

1. Wash the bones thoroughly under cold water to remove any
   trace of blood. Put them into a large pan with the rest of the
   ingredients, cover with cold water and bring to the boil. Skim
   off any scum that rises to the top.
2. Turn down the heat and simmer very gently for 30 minutes,
   skimming occasionally, then strain and it's ready to use.

How to clarify a stock
If you want a clear stock, for making a consommé,
or simply for showing off, once you've strained it,
put it back into the pan and simmer for about 5
minutes. Meanwhile, beat an egg white per litre of
stock, and drizzle it over the top of the stock. Throw
in the eggshells for good measure, simmer for a
further 5 minutes without allowing it to boil, then
take the stock off the heat and allow to stand for

about an hour. A thick foam should have risen to the top – push this aside and ladle out the stock (if you try to pour it, it will go murky again) into a sieve lined with cotton or muslin for a final strain. Ta da – it should now be completely clear!

Bright ideas for a batch of stock
Gravy, risotto, soup, Irish stew and Lancashire hot pot, daube of beef, braised celery, fennel or lettuce, boulangère potatoes, paella, fish stew . . . convinced yet?

CHAPTER 6

Baking

One of the great things about learning to cook is the sudden
realization, a year or so in, that you're actually allowed to bend the
rules — that if you're making a fish pie and you only have crème
fraîche, rather than double cream, the world's not going to fall in,
or that, even though it's not in the recipe, your sautéd spinach is
crying out for a squeeze of lemon juice and a chopped anchovy.
Experimenting is all part of the fun; casually throwing in a bit of
this, or a dollop of that, is a luxury that comes with confidence.

These days, it's very cool to be the cook who never bothers with
recipes (the implication being that genius needs no instruction)
— but with baking, you can forget everything Jamie Oliver ever
taught you, from glugs and handfuls to sinking a few beers with some
mates while you work, because if cookery is an art, this is very much a
science. Get the proportions of flour to yeast wrong in a bread
recipe, and you'll have something to prop the kitchen door open
with, but nothing for breakfast. Make your pastry too warm, and

176

you'll end up with an edible jigsaw, rather than a tart, to serve your dinner guests.

I don't mean to put you off baking — it's not difficult, as long as you read the recipe carefully, follow the measurements exactly, and don't try to be too clever. As food writer M. F. K. Fisher, who, by that point had been cooking for over thirty years, so helpfully pointed out, anyone who wants to make pastry can find comfort in the fact that, if they are not one of the lucky few to have been born with the 'inarticulate knowledge' to do so, they can at least acquire it, by reading and experimenting for themselves. End of lecture.

Perfect
Flapjacks

*F*lapjacks have an oddly wholesome reputation for something that's basically a mixture of butter and refined sugar, with a few oats chucked in to bind them together in an unholy alliance of deliciousness. Still, I'm not complaining – life can't all be *macarons* and meringues, and it's good to have a few things in your repertoire robust enough to survive being hoisted up a hill in a Barbour pocket.

There are two principal schools of flapjack: the chewy, and the crunchy. I'm firmly in the latter camp, but pleasingly the two can be  made to the same recipe; it's the cooking method that determines the texture. According to Lyle's Golden Syrup, all you need to do to turn a soft flapjack into a tooth-breaker is choose a shallower baking tray and turn the oven up. Lining it with greaseproof paper makes it easier to lift the cooked flapjacks out: all that syrup does have a tendency to be rather sticky.

The National Trust's book of *Traditional Teatime Recipes* suggests adding flour to your flapjacks, but I wouldn't – it makes them grimly stodgy, like something you might buy from a railway buffet. Jumbo oats, as recommended by Delia, give the best texture, but take a nifty tip from the internet, and cut them with easy-cook oats; it stops the finished flapjack falling apart. Pressing the mixture down firmly before baking, and allowing them to cool completely in the tin before lifting them out, also helps keep them from becoming tomorrow night's crumble topping.

Brown sugar is a must for flavour and I opt for demerara, for crunch; a generous amount of golden syrup helps on this front too. Tom Norrington-Davies gives a 'brilliantly trashy' recipe with cornflakes, in homage to his grandmother, which reminds me of the treats we used to be given at school for tidying our desks. It's unorthodox, and you may prefer to keep up the healthy pretence with seeds or dried fruit instead, but do chuck in a few handfuls one day; they lower the tone, but by golly it's fun down there.

Makes 16

300g butter, plus extra to grease
75g demerara sugar
120g golden syrup
A pinch of salt
250g jumbo rolled oats
200g quick-cook oats

1. Preheat the oven to 190°C/375°F/gas 5 (150°C/300°F/gas 2 if you prefer them chewy rather than crispy). Line a 30 x 20cm baking tin with baking parchment, cutting slits in each corner so it fits more neatly.
2. Melt the butter in a small pan with the sugar, syrup and a pinch of salt. Stir well to combine, then take off the heat and stir in the oats. Press evenly into the tin and bake for 25 minutes for chewy, 30 minutes for crunchy, until set and golden. Allow to cool completely in the tin, but cut into squares a few minutes after they come out of the oven, before they harden.

Perfect
Chocolate Brownies

Confronted by these all-American delights, the human soul crumbles into fudgey defeat, and a million eyes widen into heart-shaped pools of chocolate goo. But the dearly beloved brownie is not without its problems for the cook. For a start, there's the divisive issue of cakey versus fudgey.

The two opposing schools of thought are represented neatly by the twin deities of Nigel (Slater) and Nigella (Lawson) — the former's method is designed to incorporate as much air as possible into the batter, giving a surprisingly light, but divinely dark result, whereas the original domestic goddess concentrates on cramming as much butter as possible into her brownies, in order to ensure something quite obscenely rich and gooey. At the risk of prompting Nigella's many fans to toss away this book in disgust, her brownies are just too much for my taste — designed more for smearing saucily around the place than actually eating, perhaps.

Replacing some of the chocolate with cocoa powder, as Nigel does, ensures a rich flavour without weighing the brownies down with too much fat, and vigorous whipping of the batter helps to give them a lovely crisp crust. Plunging them straight into cold water as soon as they leave the oven, as recommended by the American First Lady of Chocolate, Alice Medrich, stops them from continuing to cook — so they stay gorgeously moist. But definitely not gooey.

250g chocolate (70% cocoa)
250g unsalted butter, softened
300g golden caster sugar
3 large free-range eggs,
     plus 1 extra egg yolk, lightly beaten
60g plain flour
½ teaspoon baking powder
A pinch of salt
60g good-quality cocoa powder
100g walnuts (optional)

1. Preheat the oven to 180°C/350°F/gas 4, and line the base and
    sides of a 23 x 23cm baking tin (a loose-bottomed one won't
    work here) with baking parchment, cutting slits in the corners to
    help it fit better.

2. Set a bowl over, but not touching, a pan of simmering water, and
    add 200g of the chocolate, broken into pieces. Allow to melt,
    stirring occasionally, then remove from the heat immediately.

3. Meanwhile, beat the butter and sugar together until light and
    fluffy, and break the rest of the chocolate into chips.

4. With the mixer still running, gradually add the eggs, beating well
    between each addition to ensure it's thoroughly incorporated
    before pouring in any more. Leave it mixing on a high speed for
    5 minutes, until the batter has a silky sheen and has increased
    in volume. Sift the flour, baking powder, salt and cocoa powder
    into a large bowl and mix well.

5. Remove the bowl from the mixer and gently fold in the melted
    chocolate and chocolate chips with a metal spoon, followed by
    the dry ingredients and walnuts.

6. Spoon the mixture into the tin, and bake for 30 minutes. Test
    with a skewer; it should come out sticky, but not coated with raw

mixture. If it does, put it back into the oven for another 3 minutes, then test again. Prepare a roasting tin of iced water.

7. When the brownies are ready, remove the tin from the oven and place in the cold water bath. Allow to cool for an hour before cutting into squares, and leave the tin in the water bath until cooled completely. Store in an airtight container: they're even better the next day.

How to melt chocolate
Chocolate is very sensitive to heat, and burns easily, so it's important to take care when melting it. You can microwave chunks of chocolate, stirring every 30 seconds until fully melted, but I find it safer to break it into a heatproof glass bowl set over a pan of simmering water, so I can keep an eye on it, and stir regularly. Don't allow the bowl to touch the water, and be careful not to drip any liquids into the chocolate or it will solidify.

Things to add to the brownies instead of walnuts
100g of pistachio nuts and the bruised seeds of
10 cardamom pods
100g of chopped toffee and 50g of roughly chopped pecans
100g of mini marshmallows
100g of fresh or frozen raspberries and 50g of white chocolate chips
125g of dried fruit — sour cherries or dried apricots are my favourites

Perfect
Shortcrust Pastry

I've never understood why people are so scared of making their own pastry. The ready-made stuff is a useful freezer standby, but if you've got forty-five minutes to spare, nothing beats the satisfaction of creating your own, and shortcrust is very even-tempered, so it's unlikely to go wrong. It's the slightly crumbly, buttery stuff you get round mince pies or under quiches, and can be made with a variety of fats depending on what you're going to use it for.

A lard and butter mixture, as used by Delia Smith, gives a savoury pastry a delectable crispness – I prefer to use all butter for my sweet shortcrust, and add an egg, rather than water, to make it a little bit richer. You can increase the amount of butter in the recipes below – Darina Allen of Ballymaloe Cookery School suggests using up to 175g for the same amount of rich shortcrust – but unless you're serving it with a very plain filling, I think this is overkill. Cold butter, as ever with pastry, is a must – put it in the freezer for fifteen minutes before you start, along with a bowl of water.

Delia pits herself against just about everyone else by recommending you bring the fat to room temperature before making the pastry – this does make it easier to rub in, but I find it more difficult to work with afterwards, so I've stuck with the traditional method here. It freezes well too, so you can make your very own convenience food.

Sweet (for fruit tarts, mince pies and so on)

225g plain white flour
2 tablespoons caster sugar
A pinch of salt
120g cold butter
1 medium free-range egg, beaten
Iced water

1. Sift the flour into a large mixing bowl and add the sugar and salt.
   Grate in the cold butter, then rub together with your fingertips
   until it resembles coarse breadcrumbs.
2. Mix the egg with 2 teaspoons of cold water, and sprinkle over
   the mixture. Mix with a table knife; you're after a coherent but
   not sticky dough, so add more water very gradually until it comes
   together.
3. Bring into a ball with your hand, then cover with clingfilm and
   refrigerate for at least 20 minutes before rolling out – 5mm is
   the usual thickness.

Savoury (for quiches, meat pies, vegetable tarts and so on)

225g plain white flour
60g cold lard, or twice
   the amount of butter below
60g cold butter
A pinch of salt
Iced water

1. Sift the flour into a large mixing bowl. Grate in the lard and butter, add a pinch of salt, and mix with your fingertips until it resembles coarse breadcrumbs.
2. Sprinkle 2 tablespoons of cold water over the mixture. Mix with a table knife; you're after a coherent but not sticky dough, so add more water very gradually until it comes together.
3. Bring into a ball with your hand, then cover with clingfilm and refrigerate for at least 20 minutes before rolling out – 5mm is the usual thickness.

The mysteries of pastry

Can I ever make pastry with my hot little hands? Although this is one of the few good things to come out of poor circulation, actually, as long as you keep everything else as cold as possible (putting the butter and water into the freezer for 15 minutes before starting is the easiest way to do this), you should achieve success, however warm your mitts are. It's important to keep the fat cold so it doesn't melt too quickly in the oven and cause the pastry to collapse.

What's the point of blind baking? Exciting as this sounds, blind baking simply means the pastry needs to be cooked before the filling is added. You must weight it down with a substitute filling, however, or it will bubble up in the heat or cave in – you can buy special ceramic balls known as baking beans or, more thriftily, you can use dried beans or even rice for the purpose; make sure you keep them in a

clearly marked jar between uses though, or someone
might be in for a disappointing dinner. Line the
pastry with foil (shiny-side down) before adding the
weights, or they'll sink in, and you'll have to pick
every single one out, which is no fun, particularly if
you're using rice (I speak from experience).

How do I know how much pastry to use? According to the
baking experts at Leiths Cookery School, to calculate
the amount of pastry you'll need for a flan ring,
you need to subtract 2 from the ring's diameter in
inches. This will give you the amount of flour to use
in ounces. For example, an 8in/20cm flan ring will
need a pastry with 6oz/170g flour, and thus 100g
butter. The recipes here should be enough for most
dishes, however — leftovers can be frozen, well-
wrapped in clingfilm, for a month or so.

How do I stop pastry from sticking to the work surface? You can
flour or lightly oil the work surface, or, if you're
really having problems (or are averse to clearing up),
roll the pastry out between two sheets of greaseproof
paper or clingfilm. This also makes it easier to
transfer it to the dish — peel one side off, use the
other one to help you guide the pastry into place,
then chill and carefully peel the rest off before use.

Perfect
Rough Puff Pastry

Life may not be too short to stuff a mushroom (had Shirley Conran never heard of Portobellos?) but it is almost certainly too brief to make your own puff pastry, particularly when this buttery flaky pastry is so much easier. If you want something even lighter, *Leiths Baking Bible* has a very clear explanation about how to attempt your own puff, but personally, my standards just aren't that high.

Rough puff is a layered pastry – which means that, like real puff, it is rolled and folded several times before cooking. It's used on the top of pies, as the vehicle for little nibbly things (cheese straws, for example), or when cooking things 'en croute', which is a fancy way of saying, 'in a pastry case'. Every layer traps air, which expands in the oven, forcing the pastry to rise – so the more folds you put in, the taller your pastry. I've gone for a simple two-stage process, but if you have the time and the inclination, you can add a few more (although beware; at some point, the flour and butter will separate, so don't go too far down this road!).

Although rough puff is a lot quicker, and easier than proper puff, there are a few rules to be followed – this is baking, after all. Don't over-mix the butter and flour – it isn't shortcrust pastry. You should still be able to see small lumps of butter in the dough when you've finished – and that butter, as usual, should be ice cold, like the water.

Lard, as used by Lindsey Bareham, does make rough puff pastry slightly crisper, but I don't think it's strictly necessary, as I prefer the flavour of butter. Delia, in contrast to most other writers, brings the pastry back up to room temperature before using it, but I'm with Michel Roux and Gordon Ramsay on this one: keeping it cold makes for taller results – and saves time. She also reckons that strong flour provides more elasticity than ordinary flour, but if it makes a difference, I can't see it, so I stick with the cheaper plain stuff.

225g plain flour
A pinch of salt
225g very cold butter
150ml iced water

1. Sift the flour and a generous pinch of salt on to a cold surface. Cut the butter into 1cm cubes and stir it in using a table knife, then gently squidge the two together, so the flour combines with the lumps of butter – the aim is not to mix it completely, so it turns into crumbs, but to have small lumps of butter coated with flour. Like the name, it should look quite rough, even unfinished.

2. Sprinkle half the water over the top and stir it in. Add enough water to bring it into a dough (unless your kitchen is very dry, you almost certainly won't need all the water), without overworking the mixture, then cover with clingfilm and refrigerate for 20 minutes.

3. Lightly flour a work surface and shape the dough into a rectangle. Roll it out until 3 times the length.

4. Fold the top third back into the centre, then bring the bottom third up to meet it, so your dough has three layers. Give the dough a quarter turn and roll out again until three times the length, fold again as before, and chill for 20 minutes before using.

Perfect
Brown Bread

*B*aking your own bread is apparently a dangerous pastime. 'Beware of making that first loaf,' cautions the late, great cookery writer Margaret Costa. 'Unless you are quite exceptionally lucky in your baker, and/or have a very easy-going family, you will find it difficult to go back to shop bread again.'

Perhaps bread has improved since those lines were written in the 1970s, but I'm a proud regular at my local loaf pushers – proper bakers deserve our support, after all. You can't beat the thrill of producing your own on occasion, though, and this nutty brown loaf is simple enough to be a weekend staple.

After testing several methods, including the unconventional approach of award-winning baker Richard Bertinet, Brittany-born author of the fabulous *Dough* (and a 'bread guru' according to the *Sunday Times*), and a more traditional technique from *Leiths Baking Bible*, as well as an overnight rise, as suggested by Delia, and Margaret Costa's no-knead loaf, I've settled upon Dan Lepard's intermittent knead technique as giving the lightest texture. (Lepard dismisses the idea that kneading develops gluten – it's all down to time apparently, which is good news, as you don't have to spend hours pummelling away.) His secret weapon? Some vitamin C, which apparently counteracts the chemical that makes so much brown bread unpalatably heavy.

A little melted butter boosts the flavour, while a proportion of white flour, as suggested by the Ballymaloe Cookery School, gives the bread a more open texture without spoiling the illusion of health. The result? A light, deliciously savoury loaf that requires very little actual work — ideal for a lazy Sunday morning.

400g strong wholemeal bread flour
50g strong white flour
2 teaspoons easy-bake yeast
  (a 7g sachet)
½ a 500mg vitamin C tablet,
  crushed
2 teaspoons salt
3 teaspoons brown sugar
400ml warm water
50g melted butter, plus a little for greasing

1. Tip the flours, yeast, vitamin powder, salt and sugar into a bowl and mix well. Add 300ml of water and stir in well, then pour in the butter and work in well. You should have a soft, sticky dough: if not, add a little more water. Cover and leave for 10 minutes.
2. Tip out on to a lightly oiled work surface and knead for 10 seconds, then put back into the bowl and cover. Repeat twice more at intervals of 10 minutes, then leave the dough to rest for 15 minutes.
3. Flatten the dough into a rough rectangle about the length of your baking tin, then roll up tightly and put into a greased 1kg loaf tin, with the join facing downwards. Cover and leave to rest in a warm place until it has doubled in height (at least 1½ hours).

4. Preheat the oven to 220°C/425°F/gas 7. Bake the bread for 20 minutes, then turn the temperature down to 200°C/400°F/gas 6 and cook for a further 15–20 minutes, until the crust is a deep brown, and the loaf sounds hollow when tapped. Turn out on to a cooling rack: don't be tempted to cut into it straight away. It may smell good, but hot bread is very difficult to digest!

How to knead
Lightly oil the work surface – this makes it much easier to clean than flour, and also prevents the dough from absorbing too much more flour and drying out. Place the ball of dough in front of you and push it away from you with the heel of your hand, shifting your weight from one side to the other as you do so. Flip the dough over with your fingertips as you bring it back towards you. Give it a quarter turn and repeat. A dough scraper is a useful tool if you make bread regularly – you can use it to pick up and portion dough, and it makes cleaning the work surface an awful lot easier.

How to store bread
Bread is best kept wrapped in paper at room temperature: plastic traps moisture and makes the crust soft, while refrigeration will dry it out.

Perfect
Fairy Cakes

(By which I mean the dainty, native sort, rather than the overgrown and brazenly blowsy cupcake which has rampaged its way across the Atlantic and into British bakeries in recent years, like some sort of garishly iced grey squirrel.)

Lightness is key with these diminutive treats – hence the addition of some extra baking powder to the self-raising flour. Make sure you beat the mixture until you can see air bubbles popping in it – the idea is to get as much air into it as possible.

Good Food magazine suggests adding some ground almonds to the batter, which helps keep the cakes nice and moist as they bake – because of their large surface area, fairy cakes are prone to dry out during cooking. Too much will make them greasy and heavy, however, so don't be tempted to increase the amount too much. I sometimes like to use a little ground rice instead, as in the *Leiths Baking Bible* recipe, which gives them a surprisingly crunchy texture.

If you're a stickler for appearances, don't fill the cases right up to the top, and allow the batter to rest for half an hour before going into the oven – this should help give you a flatter top, which is easier to decorate. According to baking expert Mich Turner, who has made cakes for everyone from the Queen to David Beckham and written several books on the subject, fairy cakes should be topped with a simple glacé icing rather than the great swirls of lurid, luscious buttercream that graces their transatlantic cousins. But I won't tell if you don't . . .

Makes 12 small cakes or 6 larger, cupcake-sized ones

85g unsalted butter, softened
85g golden caster sugar
1 medium free-range egg, at
   room temperature, beaten
100g self-raising flour, sifted
40g ground almonds
¼ teaspoon baking powder
100ml milk
150g icing sugar
Decorations such as hundreds and
   thousands or silver balls (optional)

1. Preheat the oven to 180°C/350°F/gas 4, and line a fairy cake or muffin tin with cases.
2. Cream the butter and sugar together until light and fluffy – if you do this by hand you'll need a very strong arm, so if you've got one use a food mixer on its fastest setting.
3. While continuing to mix, drizzle the egg in gradually, adding a tablespoon of flour if the mixture looks like it's about to curdle.
4. Combine the flour, almonds and baking powder, then gently fold into the mixture. Add the milk to bring the mix to a dropping consistency.
5. Divide the mixture between the cases and bake for 20 minutes

(25 for larger cupcake-sized cakes), then turn out on to a rack to cool.

6. Mix the icing sugar with a few drops of boiling water to make a thick paste, then smooth over the cooled cakes and add decorations before it sets. Eat quickly — fairy cakes don't keep!

Perfect
Scones

Ah, the Great British scone. Such an innocuous looking little thing – plain really, in comparison with the monstrous American muffin, or the gaudy *macaron* – yet how much more precious than these more fashionable baked goods. The honest scone has no sugary icing or exotically perfumed ganache to hide behind – it stands or falls on its absolute freshness, which is why it's impossible to purchase a good example on the high street. You will never get a better scone than a homemade scone.

Every scone maker aspires to the towering triumphs of the soufflé – the miraculous transformation of lumpen flour and fat into a billowing cloud of fluffy dough – but all too often ends up with stubbornly flat biscuits instead. The secret, learnt from the unnervingly wholesome Irish celebrity chef Rachel Allen, is using a raising agent (bicarbonate of soda and cream of tartar) and super-fine flour. Both Rachel and Marcus Wareing put eggs in their scones, but I find this makes them rather rich and cakey – being of

a puritanical bent, I prefer the lard scones in the National Trust's book of *Traditional Teatime Recipes*, which are feather-light, and savoury enough to really justify all that cream and jam. If you prefer a sweeter scone, you can add 25g of caster sugar to the mixture after rubbing the fat into the flour.

River Cottage baker Dan Stevens cautions against overworking the dough, and Delia believes success lies in pushing, rather than twisting the cutter – both tips that seem to help give a slightly better rise. If you really want billowing scones, gently pat the dough down, rather than rolling it out – it gives slightly unruly, wild-looking results, but at least no one will be in any doubt that they're homemade. Top with rich, salty West Country butter, a slick of ruby red jam and a thick dollop of clotted cream, in whatever order takes your fancy – just make sure there's plenty of them!

Makes 6

350g super-fine '00' flour,
   plus extra to dust
1 heaped teaspoon
   bicarbonate of soda
2 heaped teaspoons cream of tartar
A pinch of salt
50g chilled butter, plus extra to grease
50g chilled lard (or double the
   quantity of butter above)
130ml milk, plus 1 tablespoon to glaze

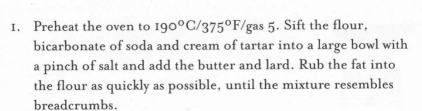

1. Preheat the oven to 190°C/375°F/gas 5. Sift the flour, bicarbonate of soda and cream of tartar into a large bowl with a pinch of salt and add the butter and lard. Rub the fat into the flour as quickly as possible, until the mixture resembles breadcrumbs.
2. Gradually add enough milk to create a soft dough, and bring together into a ball. Very gently roll or press out on a floured

surface until about 2.5cm thick, then cut into rounds using a 7cm cutter lightly dusted with flour, being careful not to twist the cutter. Bring any remaining dough together and repeat the process until it is all used up.

3. Place on a lightly buttered baking tray, and brush the tops with milk. Bake for about 15 minutes, until well risen and golden on top, then cool slightly on a wire rack and eat as soon as possible.

Perfect
Victoria Sandwich

*T*his queen of the tea table can, in my opinion, never be toppled by any chocolate-flavoured pretender – and Hugh Fearnley-Whittingstall, who's won first prize for his Victoria sandwich in his local village fête, agrees, calling it one of the finest cakes ever to grace a plate. Although it's often spoken of as such, strictly speaking, it's not a sponge at all – according to Mary Berry, a true sponge is a whisked mixture of eggs, sugar and flour; the kind of thing one would make a Swiss roll from in fact, rather than an honest British doorstop of a cake.

It wasn't until the development of baking powder in the 1840s that butter could be added to cake mixtures without weighing them down in the oven. This fabulous new invention was celebrated with an appropriately patriotic cake – although anyone making Mrs Beeton's first recipe would have been left scratching their heads, as the original domestic goddess (recently revealed as a remarkably astute plagiarist in Kathryn Hughes' biography) forgot to include the eggs.

The same general principles apply as with the fairy cakes above, but you can afford to be a little more generous with the eggs, and dispense with the ground almonds, as bigger cakes are less prone to drying out during cooking. I'm with Hugh on insisting on raspberry jam in my sandwich – it's something about the gritty texture of the seeds — but if you're feeling particularly decadent, you can add clotted cream, or butter cream (a mixture of softened butter and icing sugar) as well. Just don't forget the eggs.

115g butter, softened, plus
    extra to grease
115g caster sugar, plus
    1 tablespoon extra to serve
2 medium free-range eggs, at
    room temperature, beaten
115g self-raising flour, sifted
1 teaspoon baking powder
2 tablespoons milk
3 tablespoons raspberry jam, to serve

1. Preheat the oven to 180°C/350°F/gas 4. Grease two 15cm sandwich tins with butter and line the bases with baking parchment.

2. Cream the butter and sugar together in a mixing bowl or food mixer until light and very fluffy. Very gradually add the eggs, beating well between each addition, so the mixture doesn't curdle — if it threatens to do so, fold in a tablespoon of flour before adding the rest of the egg.

3. Sift the flour and baking powder together, then fold the flour and milk into the creamed mixture to give a batter loose enough to fall from the spoon when you give it a sharp shake. Divide the mixture evenly between the two tins, smooth the tops with the back of a spoon, and put them into the oven for about 20 minutes, until they're well risen and golden, and the edges have started to shrink away from the sides — keep an eye on them for the last 5 minutes of cooking.

4. Allow to cool in the tins for a few minutes, then run a table knife round the edges to loosen them and gently tip the cakes on to a wire rack. Leave to cool completely – if you add jam when the cakes are warm, it will melt.

5. Choose the flatter of the two sponges, and top with a thick layer of jam. If it's annoyingly pointy, you can cheat and cut a little bit off so the two will stick together better. Sandwich the two cakes together, and dust the top with caster sugar.

Perfect
Mince Pies

I realized a couple of years ago that, after the excitement of the first dozen or so, I didn't really much care for most mince pies. They're oddly sour and gloopy, with the kind of stodgy, sugary pastry that weighs on festive merriment like lead. The beauty of making your own, apart from the fact that it's possibly the very best way to get yourself in the Christmas mood, is that you can customize them to your taste.

 Let's tackle the mincemeat first, which is usually a mix of dried vine fruits, mixed peel and apple base. Leiths' mincemeat includes a chopped banana, which adds a surprisingly subtle sweetness to the mix, but means that the mincemeat has to be used immediately, so the flavours don't have a chance to really develop.

Delia's recipe has a similarly unusual addition — fresh cranberries, to add some 'sharp acidity' to the mixture. Rather too much of it, in my opinion — cranberries are indeed very bitter. Her recipe also differs from the rest by gently cooking the mincemeat for 3 hours to melt the suet. This, she says, coats the apple, and stops it fermenting. It does, however, make the mixture look pretty ugly, so unless you're planning on keeping the mincemeat for a few months, it probably isn't worth it.

Mrs Beeton, of course, uses real mince in her mincemeat — lean rump steak, to be precise. It has novelty value, but I can't really see that such a small amount adds much to the pies themselves, apart from making people oddly nervous — and it has to be matured for two weeks, by which time the beef is impossible to distinguish from the rest of the ingredients. Thank God.

The *Ballymaloe Cookery Course* mincemeat, matriarch Myrtle Allen's family recipe, calls for the apple to be baked before it's stirred into the rest of the ingredients. I don't like the smoother texture this gives the mincemeat, or the breakfasty flavour that the marmalade she uses imparts, but whisky is, I have to agree, a much nicer idea than brandy — it has a more assertive booziness which seems appropriate at this time of year. Feel free to tinker with the mix of dried fruit and nuts in the recipe below — if you often find mincemeat too sweet, for example, substitute sour cherries for the glacé ones.

If you've made the mincemeat, then you may as well go the whole hog and knock up some pastry as well — the admiration you'll receive is utterly disproportionate to the actual work involved. Nigella's flaky pastry is too greasy for mince pies, I find — crumbly shortcrust works better, particularly if you're not going to scoff them all straight from the oven. Christmas deserves better than workaday plain shortcrust though: instead, replace some of the flour with ground almonds, as Leiths do, and add a little orange flower water, like Nigella, to make the case as tasty as the filling.

Listening to a Radio 4 phone-in while baking last Christmas, I heard mention of a family tradition I rather liked the sound of. The caller filled one mince pie every year with English mustard, turning every teatime over the festive period into a Russian roulette until the rogue pie was discovered – not a game for those with weak hearts, apparently, but a nice way to inject some danger into the cosiest season of the year.

Makes 24 pies (800g mincemeat)

For the mincemeat
50g each sultanas, raisins, currants,
    finely chopped mixed peel
50g each dried figs and glacé
    cherries, finely chopped
1 piece stem ginger, finely chopped,
    plus 1 tablespoon of its syrup
25g each almonds and pecans, finely chopped
200g dark muscovado sugar
½ teaspoon mixed spice
3 tablespoons whisky
2 tablespoons suet or cold grated butter
Zest of 1 lemon, finely grated
1 small unpeeled cooking apple, coarsely grated

For the pastry
340g plain flour
A pinch of salt
225g cold butter
85g ground almonds
100g golden caster sugar
2 egg yolks
1 teaspoon orange blossom water or orange juice
Beaten egg or milk, to glaze
Icing sugar, to dust

1. Mix together the mincemeat ingredients and ideally put into sterilized jars to mature for at least a fortnight or up to a year, shaking occasionally; you can use it immediately, but it will be even better if the flavours are given a chance to blend.

2. To make the pastry, sieve the flour into a mixing bowl with a pinch of salt. Grate in the butter, and rub into the mixture until it resembles coarse breadcrumbs. Stir in the ground almonds and sugar.

3. Mix the egg yolks with the orange blossom water and 1½ tablespoons of ice-cold water. Add enough to the mixture to bring it together into a firm, but not wet dough when stirred with a knife. Shape into a ball by hand, wrap in clingfilm, and chill for half an hour.

4. Preheat the oven to 190°C/375°F/gas 5. Grease your tartlet tins with butter, and roll out half the pastry on a floured surface until about 3mm thick. Using a 7cm round cutter, cut out bases to line the tartlet tins. Fill each three-quarters full with mincemeat, then roll out the other half of the pastry and cut out lids, using a 6cm round cutter. Dampen the edge with a little water or milk, and press down lightly on the pies to seal. Brush the tops with water or beaten egg, and prick the tops with a fork.

5. Bake for about 20 minutes, until golden, then leave to cool in the tins for 5 minutes before lifting out on to a wire rack. Dust with icing sugar to serve.

Fancy pies
If you have the right-shaped cutter, you can top the pies with a pastry star instead of a lid – or one made out of marzipan. You can also adapt

the crumble topping on page 221 to make a more
unusual mince pie topping: try adding a couple
of tablespoons of flaked almonds, a pinch of
cinnamon or the zest of ½ an orange. Minimalists,
however, might want to simply set a single glacé
cherry, or blanched whole almond, in the middle
of the mincemeat in mini mince pies — why, they
practically count as a health food.

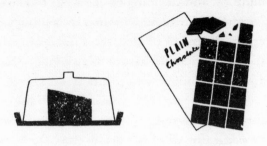

CHAPTER 7

Puddings

Ah, puddings. The point where cooks reap their sweet reward – because not only are they a pleasure to cook, as well as eat, but their capacity to charm will leave you pleasurably imprisoned in a perfect storm of admiration and gratitude. People may compliment your canapés, or politely praise your *pommes purée*, but dessert – that's the moment when you win their hearts. (They have other attractions for the chef too; the fact that you can keep tasting them, ever so conscientiously, as you go along not least among them.)

I don't think it's alarmingly jingoistic to admit that I think the British make some of the finest puddings in the world. In *English Foods*, Jane Grigson quotes one glorious seventeenth-century French convert on the subject: 'They bake them in an oven, they boil them . . . they make them fifty several ways: BLESSED BE HE THAT INVENTED PUDDING, for it is a manna that hits the palates of all sorts of people.' However, I'm willing to admit that other countries do have their moments; the French being particularly good at fancy dinner party puddings, and the Italians, as Elizabeth David notes, specializing in 'very showy' things 'drenched in sweet liqueur' or 'smothered in cream'. Hence I've included a few more exotic recipes in here, for that odd moment when crumble and custard just won't cut the mustard.

My favourite sources of inspiration for sweet things are Mary Norwak's *English Puddings*, for all things traditional, the works of Nigella Lawson, when a spot of unembarrassed over-indulgence is called for, and Jane Grigson's *Fruit Book*, for more virtuous moments. Occasionally, of course, I come over all Nigel Slater, and fancy nothing more than a stickily ripe peach — but even then, it's nice to know that there's ice cream in the freezer as well. Just in case.

Perfect
Tiramisù

As it was originally intended, tiramisù, or 'pick me up' as it's generally translated, is a perfect shot of sugar and caffeine to propel you out into the night after a monumental Italian feast. Unfortunately, you'd be hard-pressed to pick up much more than your pyjamas after the English translation of the dish – and you'd better hope they have an elasticated waistband. Laden with cream cheese, gelatine and crème fraîche (I'm looking at you, Gordon Ramsay), double cream (step up, Heston) and even condensed milk (hang your head, Phil Vickery), they're definitely not the kind of desserts to chase down a lasagne, or an osso buco.

Tiramisù is usually made with eggs – yolks to add richness to the mascarpone cheese, and whites to give it volume. Jamie Oliver gives a recipe for a 'quick' eggless version, which is topped with vanilla-infused mascarpone. I'm not sure about the vanilla, or the orange juice he adds to his sponge finger base, but I do like his idea of whisking some vin santo, or Italian dessert wine, into the rather blandly sweet mascarpone. The classic Italian cookbook *The Silver Spoon* gives a more traditional, custardy recipe, which, although lighter than many creamy British versions, is still very rich – I prefer Angela Hartnett's Auntie Maria's version, which has a higher ratio of eggs to mascarpone, giving a topping which is more like a mousse than a cream.

She reckons the secret is boudoir biscuits soaked in strong coffee, with a hefty dose of booze to cut through the sweetness above. I've added a little sugar to the coffee and brandy, and a subtle dash of nutty liqueur to the topping, but more austere palates might want to leave one or both of these out. Lady fingers, savoiardi or boudoir biscuits are the same sponge fingers you might use as a trifle base – look in the baking or cake section of your local supermarket.

Serves 6

1 x 175g packet of sponge fingers
130g caster sugar
200ml freshly brewed strong
   black coffee, cooled
25ml brandy
4 large free-range eggs
150g mascarpone, at room temperature
30ml Frangelico or liqueur of your choice
50g dark chocolate, to grate

1. Arrange the sponge fingers in one layer in the bottom of a large, but relatively shallow serving dish, measuring roughly 32 x 26cm – you may have to break them up to fit them round the edges. Stir 30g of caster sugar into the coffee, then add the brandy. Pour over the sponge fingers.
2. Separate the eggs, and beat the yolks together with the 100g of caster sugar until they pale and double in volume, which should take about 3 minutes with electric beaters and rather longer by hand. Whisk in the mascarpone, and, when smooth, drizzle in the liqueur very gradually, whisking well to combine.

3. Whisk the egg whites until they form stiff peaks, then fold into the mascarpone mixture very slowly and gently. Spoon over the top of the fingers, and gently smooth the top. Refrigerate for at least a couple of hours, and top with grated chocolate just before serving.

Perfect
New York Cheesecake

*T*here are two very different types of dessert rejoicing in the name of cheesecake: one baked, and one chilled. This recipe for the classic New York-style baked dessert is therefore bound to disappoint some people, but I'd urge you to give it a try nevertheless. Nigella whisks in egg whites to make her cheesecake fluffy, but I prefer a wobbly, creamy texture.

I've always found the traditional cream cheese and egg recipe rather claggy — indeed, that seems to be part of their attraction (Delia has a good recipe if you like your cheesecakes to stick to the roof of your mouth) — but if you cut the mixture with cream you'll get a smoother, lighter result. I use soured cream, which gives a lovely tanginess to the filling, and a little vanilla extract and lemon zest to subtly flavour it; you really don't need anything else, I promise. It should still be slightly undercooked in the middle — if you leave it in the oven to cool, it's less likely to crack on top.

Lindy's, the Broadway deli so famous for its cheesecakes that they get a mention in the classic New York musical *Guys and Dolls*, uses a pastry crust, but a mixture of crumbly digestives and crunchy ginger nuts gives a much more interesting flavour and texture. I also quite like crushed Oreo biscuits, but it's often difficult to leave enough uneaten to work with, so, for a slightly cheaper chocolate hit, add a layer of melted chocolate to the base and allow to cool before adding the topping.

As well as providing flavour, chocolate can also act as a handy barrier between the topping and the base, helping to keep it crunchy – many recipes I've tried suffer from slightly soggy bottoms, which comes as a bit of a let-down, however delicious and creamy the topping. On a non-chocolate cheesecake, however, this can also be rectified by pre-baking the base in a hot oven, and then brushing it with egg white, which will set to form a film – a bit fiddly, but well worth it.

Cheesecakes are surprisingly fragile things at the best of times, so make life easier for yourself by investing in a springform tin – one of the ones with a separate upper, which is fastened with a spring – or you'll be hard-pressed to get the thing out in one piece.

> 60g digestive biscuits (4 biscuits)
> 60g ginger nuts (6 biscuits)
> 50g butter
> A pinch of salt
> 600g full-fat cream cheese,
>   at room temperature
> 200g soured cream
> 4 tablespoons cornflour
> 150g caster sugar
> Zest of ½ a lemon, finely grated
> 1 teaspoon vanilla extract
> 4 large free-range eggs, at room
>   temperature, plus 1 egg white

1. Preheat the oven to 180°C/350°F/gas 4 and put a baking sheet on the middle shelf. Crush the biscuits by putting them into a freezer bag and hitting them with a rolling pin – you want to

leave some larger chunks in there, so this is better than using a food processor. Melt the butter in a small pan, then add the crumbs and a pinch of salt and mix well.

2. Spread the crumbs over the base of a 20cm cake tin, 6cm tall (springform if you have one), and press down firmly with a glass until you have a firm, flat base. Put the tin into the hot oven for 20 minutes while you make the topping.

3. Put the cheese into a large bowl and stir with a whisk to soften it and get rid of any lumps. Mix in the soured cream, cornflour, sugar, lemon zest and vanilla extract. Beat the whole eggs together, and then add them to the mixture, little by little, then beat just until the mixture is smooth.

4. Take the tin out of the oven and brush the surface of the base lightly with egg white. Turn the oven down to 110°C/225°F/gas ¼, and keep the door open for a couple of minutes to help it to cool.

5. Leave the base for a few minutes while the oven cools, then pour the mixture into the tin, and shake gently to level it. You can run your finger gently over the top to get rid of any air bubbles. Put on the hot baking sheet and bake for 1½ hours, until set, but still slightly wobbly. Run a thin spatula around the edge to separate the cake from the tin, then turn the oven off and allow the cheesecake to cool completely inside before taking it out, removing from the tin and refrigerating.

Cheat: if your cheesecake cracks on top, cover it with fresh fruit, or fruit compote or coulis (see page 214), just before serving and no one will ever know the difference.

Simple fruit coulis

Take 500g of soft fruit (peaches, strawberries, apricots, blackcurrants — whatever happens to be in season) and remove any stems or stones. Chop larger fruit roughly, and then put into a blender with 300g of caster sugar and whiz to a purée. Taste and add more sugar if the fruit needs it, then keep refrigerated until ready to use.

Perfect
Apple Pie

More proof, if it were needed, that the simplest dishes are often the tastiest, this never fails to disappoint. The Americans seem to have stolen the rights somewhere along the line, only to restyle it as some sort of national fetish, but we all know that only one country makes a decent pie – although we can't blame them for trying. Interestingly, since those first brave settlers crossed the ocean with a pocketful of pips, our recipes have diverged – the American version retains the pastry shell of medieval pies (much like our own pork pie in form, if not flavour), while over here, the fashion since the seventeenth century has been a simple pastry topping. The French, meanwhile, saucy as ever, favour a topless *tarte aux pommes*, garnished with rows of fussily sliced apple and glazed with jelly, but then they're content to leave the hard work to the pâtisserie.

Back to the king of pies. A sweet, crisp shortcrust is perfect here – using a puff pastry, as bearded celebrity chef Antony Worrall Thompson recommends, seems overly fancy somehow. Nigella cooks her apples briefly in butter and sugar before adding them to the pie dish, which gives a very sweet, caramelized finish more suited to a tarte Tatin than an honest British apple pie – instead, coat them with butter in the dish itself, for a gorgeously rich, but defiantly appley filling.

The mixture of dessert and cooking apples is, like the butter, an idea borrowed from Jane Grigson's *English Food*, and gives a more interesting flavour to the filling. This way I don't think it needs cinnamon, or ginger, or any of the other adornments suggested by Delia, Jamie and all the rest, but if you do, by all means add them along with the sugar.

Serves 6

I quantity of shortcrust pastry
  (see page 183)
600g cooking apples (about
  2 medium Bramleys)
300g dessert apples – Cox's Orange
  Pippins are ideal here
125g butter
125g golden caster sugar, plus extra to dust
I egg, beaten with I teaspoon water

1. Preheat the oven to 180°C/350°F/gas 4 and put a baking tray on the middle shelf. While the pastry is chilling, peel and core the apples and cut into 2–3cm chunks. Put them into a 20cm pie dish. (Don't do this too far in advance or they will discolour.)
2. Melt the butter in the microwave, or a small pan, and stir in the sugar. Pour over the apples and mix well. Brush the rim of the pie dish with beaten egg.
3. Roll out the pastry on a floured surface until about 5mm thick. Roll it around your pin, and then unroll it on top of the pie, pressing it around the rim and cutting off any excess. Brush the

top with egg, sprinkle with sugar, then cut a small hole in the centre to allow the steam to escape.

4. Put on the baking tray and bake for about 45 minutes, until golden. Serve with ice cream (see page 230) or custard (see page 218).

Tarting up your pie

Use any extra pastry to make an apple shape (or anything else you might fancy seeing on the top of your pie) and fix to the pastry using the egg wash. Alternatively, if you're feeling particularly fancy, you can make a lattice top for your pie. Cut the rolled pastry into strips about 1cm wide. Brush the rim of the dish with egg wash, and cover it with pastry strips, laid end to end all the way round, cutting off any excess. Brush again with egg wash, and then lay pastry strips in parallel across the width of the dish, leaving a gap between each so you can see the filling, and pressing them firmly down on the pastry rim at each end to secure. Brush with egg wash, then arrange a second layer of strips across the dish at an approximate 45° angle to the first to give a criss-cross effect. Trim off any excess, then put a second layer of pastry strips all the way round the rim and brush the whole lot with egg wash.

Perfect
Custard

*Y*ou really can't beat a jug of rich yellow custard. The perfect partner for an apple crumble, the only topping for a trifle, and, at its simplest, utterly divine poured over a sliced banana, it's a recipe to master. I must confess to undimmed affection for lumpy Bird's, but if you're after the proper stuff, this beats the gloopy ready-made supermarket versions hands down.

Delia's Proper Custard Sauce uses cornflour to help stabilize the mixture, and, as it starts off with double cream, only takes a couple of minutes to thicken in the pan — it's absurdly easy, and great for knocking up on a custard whim, but although luxuriously creamy, is too bland to go with anything special. Upping the egg content, and using whole milk instead, lets you in for a whole lot more stirring, but the result has a delicious silky richness that makes it worthwhile.

The important thing when making custard is to keep it cool — it will curdle if it gets too hot — so I've tried making it in a bowl suspended above a pan of simmering water, as suggested by Tom Norrington-Davies in *Just Like Mother Used to Make*, but as long as it's made in a thick-bottomed pan, and over a very low heat, it's an unnecessary precaution. I've included the instructions below, though, for the faint of heart.

Serves 6 (makes 600ml)

568ml whole milk
1 vanilla pod, slit in half and
   seeds scraped out
6 egg yolks
2 tablespoons caster sugar
1 tablespoon cornflour

1. Put the milk into a thick-bottomed pan with the vanilla pod and seeds on a gentle heat. Stir, then bring the milk to just below a simmer; do not allow it to boil.
2. Meanwhile, beat the egg yolks, sugar and cornflour together in a large bowl.
3. Remove the vanilla pod from the hot milk and pour the milk on to the yolk and sugar mixture, stirring all the time.
4. Turn the heat down as low as it will go, and pour the custard back into the pan. Stirring slowly and continuously, cook until it coats the back of a wooden spoon – the longer you cook it, the thicker it will be. Alternatively, if you're not feeling terribly brave, suspend a heatproof bowl over a pan of simmering water, pour the yolk and milk mixture into that, and proceed as above. Bear in mind you'll be tied to the stove for about 15 minutes, so put some good music on.
5. Decant into a jug and, if you're not using it immediately and dislike custard skin, press some clingfilm on to the surface to prevent one forming.

TIP

Custard know-how

To see whether custard is cooked,
lift the wooden spoon out of the
pan and run your finger down the
back — if it leaves a clear line in the
custard, it's thick enough to serve.

To rescue curdled custard, take it
off the heat immediately and strain it through a
fine sieve, then whiz in a blender until smooth —
depending on how bad the situation is, you may
then be able to add it to a milk and cornflour paste
and reheat it as normal. Or you may have to start
again. Sorry.

Custards aren't just for pudding — one of the
signature dishes at Rowley Leigh's Café Anglais is a
baked Parmesan custard, served with anchovy toast.
Find the recipe online.

Vanilla is just one flavour of custard: try infusing yours
with nutmeg, star anise or a cinnamon stick instead.

Bird's custard was invented by a Birmingham
chemist in 1837 to please his wife, who was allergic
to eggs. Now that's love.

Baked custards, such as crème brûlée, crème caramel
and the classic British custard tart, use the same
basic recipe (although crème brûlée is generally
enriched with double cream rather than milk) but
the custard thickens in the oven rather than in the
pan. It's advisable to cook them in a bain-marie,
or water bath, for a really silky texture — the same
applies to bread and butter pudding.

Perfect
Crumble

Crumble is the ultimate childhood pudding: hot, sweet, and incredibly comforting. It took me nearly two decades to make something that matched up to the stuff we scoffed at school. Dot the dinner lady, I salute you – how I wish I'd asked for the recipe, instead of just seconds.

Interestingly, *The Oxford Companion to Food* suggests that crumble probably originated in the Second World War, as a quicker, easier alternative to pastry, and would have originally used whatever fat was available at the time. These days, butter is de rigueur, but sprinkling over a little water, as suggested by Nigel Slater in his *Real Fast Puddings*, helps to bind the mixture together – Nigella Lawson cleverly freezes the topping before cooking it, which slows down the melting of the butter, and gives the baked crumble a more craggy texture.

To boost the flavour, Mary Norwak, author of *English Puddings*, suggests using light brown sugar. This imparts a rather sandy texture, so I compromise with a mixture of this and crunchy demerara, and also substitute some of the flour with ground almonds, although not quite so much as Jane Grigson recommends, as I find this makes it a bit spongy, like a cobbler. You can also add a few handfuls of oats on top, and a little ground ginger or cinnamon if you like.

Serves 4

100g plain flour
50g ground almonds
125g chilled, unsalted butter, cut
   into cubes
35g demerara sugar
35g caster sugar, plus extra for the fruit as required
About 900g fresh fruit, stoned or cored as necessary and cut
   into chunks — cooking apples should be softened in a pan
   with a tablespoon of water and a little sugar first
Handful of porridge oats/chopped nuts (optional)

1. Preheat the oven to 200°C/400°F/gas 6. Combine the flour, ground almonds and butter in a food processor or large bowl, and pulse briefly, or rub with your fingertips, until the mixture resembles very coarse breadcrumbs, with a few larger lumps. Add the sugars and stir through.
2. Sprinkle with a little cold water and rake through with a fork until you have a lumpy, crumbly mixture. Put this into the freezer for 10 minutes, or, if making ahead, into the fridge until you're ready to bake.
3. Meanwhile, put your prepared fruit in a lightly greased, shallow baking dish, and sprinkle with sugar — taste it first to see how much you think it needs. You can also add any spices at this point (½ teaspoon of ground cinnamon or ginger, for example, for apples or plums).
4. Arrange the crumble over the top of the fruit — don't press it down — and now is the time to sprinkle with oats or nuts if you are inclined. Bake for about 30 minutes, until golden and bubbling, and cool slightly before serving.

Perfect
Sticky Toffee Pudding

STP, as us aficionados know it (or maybe that's just me), sounds like the ultimate school dinner staple; heavy, gooey and unapologetically sweet, it's just the thing to set you up for a game of lacrosse, a page of trig, and assorted other jolly wheezes. But you won't find Enid Blyton's schoolgirls tucking into sticky toffee pud after lights out, or Billy Bunter scoffing the stuff from his tuckbox, because, as every food nerd knows, it was invented in the 1970s by Francis Coulson of the Lake District's Sharrow Bay Hotel.

Mr Coulson may well have been even better at publicity than he was at puddings, however, because according to Simon Hopkinson, the late and 'legendary' chef once admitted to him that he'd adapted the idea from one Mrs Martin of Lancashire. Some years later, this good lady's son contacted Hopkinson to tell him she'd been given the recipe by a Canadian friend, which makes sticky toffee pudding about as British as flipper pie. No matter, wherever it comes from, I'm glad it made the trip.

Coulson's recipe, as recorded by Gary Rhodes (who, in an audacious attempt at thickening the plot, bills it as 'a good old English pudding which is made all over the country'), uses chopped dates, softened in boiling water, and folded into creamed butter and sugar, along with eggs, self-raising flour and vanilla essence. Stolen or not, I prefer it to Hopkinson's updated version, which blends the dates to a purée, and mixes everything together in one go — whatever Simon says about all that careful creaming being destroyed by the hot water, Coulson's recipe still rises higher than his, and boasts a more interesting texture.

Ever modish, young Jamie Oliver makes his STP with yoghurt, which keeps it moist, but weighs the batter down — and his cornucopia of sweet spices gives the whole thing a gingerbread flavour. I've restricted myself to a sober pinch of cloves, to complement the dates without overpowering them, and added walnuts, instead of Delia's pecans, to give the dish a bit of crunch: this is one dish sweet enough to stand up to their bitterness.

As always, some people don't know when to leave well alone: Tamasin Day-Lewis offers a steamed version with apricots in her *All You Can Eat* compendium, claiming the fruit's acidic sharpness works better with the dish's signature toffee sauce. I find them jarring — and as for steaming, one may as well try and grill a brownie.

I like Jamie's simple toffee sauce better than all the creamy, butterscotchy varieties which appear to have been inspired by Francis Coulson's 'original' version, but it strikes me that I'm missing a trick by simply drizzling it on top of the pudding. Lining the dish with a layer of sauce, and then putting it into the freezer to firm it up while making the batter (a trick I must confess to have stolen myself, from the internet), yields sticky deliciousness all the way through — this is one transatlantic migrant which will have no problem getting its visa renewed.

Serves 6

175g medjool dates, stoned and roughly chopped
I teaspoon bicarbonate of soda
300ml boiling water
50g unsalted butter, softened
80g golden caster sugar
80g dark muscovado sugar
2 large free-range eggs, beaten
175g plain flour
I teaspoon baking powder
A pinch of ground cloves
A pinch of salt
75g walnut halves, roughly chopped

For the sauce
115g unsalted butter
75g golden caster sugar
40g dark muscovado sugar
140ml double cream
A pinch of salt

1. Preheat the oven to 180°C/350°F/gas 4. Butter a deep baking dish approximately 24 x 24cm.

2. Make the sauce by putting all the ingredients into a pan and heating slowly until the butter has melted, then turn up the heat and bring to the boil. Boil for about 4 minutes, until the sauce has thickened enough to coat the back of a spoon. Pour half the sauce into the base of the dish and put it into the freezer.

3. Put the dates and bicarbonate of soda into a heatproof dish and

cover with the boiling water. Leave to soften while you prepare the rest of the pudding.

4. Beat together the butter and both sugars until fluffy, and then beat in the eggs, a little at a time. Sift in the flour, baking powder, cloves and a pinch of salt until well combined, then add the dates and their soaking water, and the walnuts, and mix well.

5. Take the baking dish out of the freezer and pour the batter on top of the toffee sauce. Put into the oven for 30 minutes, until firm to the touch, then take out of the oven and heat the grill to medium.

6. Poke a few small holes evenly over the surface of the pudding with a skewer or fork, and pour over the rest of the sauce. Put briefly under the grill, keeping an eye on it as it burns easily. Serve with vanilla ice cream.

Perfect
Chocolate Mousse

*C*rêpes suzettes and rhum baba may have come and gone, and profiteroles long outstayed their welcome, but chocolate mousse is one 60s favourite that's immune to the vagaries of fashion. Richly flavoured, yet light as air, there are few more perfect ways to end a meal.

The classic recipe comes from Elizabeth David. Her simple chocolate mousse, in *French Provincial Cooking*, is just that – an egg, and an ounce of chocolate (or, less neatly, 30g), per person, turned into something quite, quite magical. You don't need to add butter, like Julia Child, or double cream, like Gordon Ramsay – they'll just weigh down the mixture and dilute its flavour, and fiddling around with an Italian meringue, like Franco-American chef Daniel Boulud, is just a waste of time. The reluctantly health-conscious might be interested to hear that Raymond Blanc's egg-white-only version is surprisingly good, although it does inevitably lack the richness of the whole-egg recipes.

David's mousse, brought up to date for modern tastes with a little sugar, is unbeatably simple and delicious. The beauty of it is that you can play around with flavourings to suit your own taste – add more sugar, or leave it out completely, pop in a teaspoon of coffee, or booze (whisky, rum, Grand Marnier – whatever you fancy), a

sprinkle of chilli flakes or a few cardamom seeds – just make sure
you work quickly, and with a light hand, and you have one of the
easiest, and most fashionably retro puddings around.

Makes 2

**60g plain chocolate
    (at least 70% cocoa)
2 medium free-range eggs
2 teaspoons caster sugar (or to taste)**

1. Break the chocolate into pieces and put it into a bowl over, but
   not touching, a pan of simmering water. When the chocolate
   begins to melt, turn the heat off. Separate the eggs.
2. Whisk the egg whites into soft peaks, then add the sugar, and
   whisk briefly.
3. Mix the egg yolks quickly into the melted chocolate and then
   whisk in a third of the egg white. Fold the rest very gently into
   the mixture until just combined (be careful not to over-mix),
   then put into two serving bowls and refrigerate for at least 4
   hours, until set.

- -

Chocolate-only chocolate mousse
Vegans, or the inquisitive of mind, might be
interested in the 'Chocolate Chantilly' recipe of
French culinary chemist Hervé This, which calls
for chocolate to be melted with water over a low
heat, then whisked up into an intensely rich,

dairy-free cream while the mixture is cooling in a bowl of iced water. It's amazing stuff. His book *Molecular Gastronomy* is a useful adjunct to *McGee on Food and Cooking*, a masterpiece which anyone seriously interested in cookery would do well to invest in — although, at 883 pages, it's perhaps not one you should feel too guilty about dipping in and out of.

Perfect
Vanilla Ice Cream

I don't know much about international diplomacy, but I do have a sneaking suspicion that it probably doesn't make enough use of ice cream. There's something innocently joyful about the stuff — how can anyone be angry when holding a double cone with a flake on top?

Ice cream is too light-hearted a foodstuff for snobbery — even the much-derided Mr Whippy can raise a smile on a hot day — but it is worth making yourself, for two reasons. The first is that, as yet, even the poshest supermarkets don't tend to stock the esoteric flavour combinations that ice cream is such a great showcase for (plum and Earl Grey, from Morfudd Richards' fabulous book, *Lola's Ice Creams and Sundaes*, is my current favourite). Secondly, and perhaps more importantly, people tend to be really, really impressed when you serve homemade ice cream.

Before you can go mad with the anchovy palate cleansers, however, it's important to master some basic principles. Heston Blumenthal, a self-professed 'ice cream fanatic', explains that all ice creams are made of five key ingredients: ice crystals, fat, sugar, air and 'other solids', including the proteins and minerals contained in the milk. Most will also include an emulsifier, such as xanthan gum (in the case of mass-produced ice cream) or egg yolk, in more traditional recipes. Only the simplest, 'Philadelphia-style' ices, which are really just flavoured creams, scorn stabilizers — they're meltingly light, but rather gritty.

Most other ice creams start off with some sort of custard base — the more eggs, the richer the flavour, although I find, after some experimentation, that you can go too far down that road; you should be able to eat a big bowlful if the mood takes you. My big breakthrough came when I took a tip from Heston himself, and added skimmed milk powder in place of the double cream that weighs down so many more traditional recipes — it may sound less appetizing, but it's a clever way of giving the ice cream body without making it heavy. The recipe below is much less rich than his version, however — more suitable for a summer afternoon in the garden than an evening at the Fat Duck — and all the better with strawberries for it in my opinion. An ice cream maker will make your life a lot easier, particularly if you develop a taste for your own creations, but it's not essential.

2 vanilla pods
4 large free-range egg yolks
568ml whole milk
50g skimmed milk powder
90g caster sugar

1. Slit the vanilla pods open with a knife and scrape out the seeds. Put the seeds into a food mixer with the egg yolks.
2. Pour the milk into a large pan and add the empty vanilla pods, the skimmed milk powder and 2 teaspoons of sugar. Whisk to mix thoroughly, and bring to the boil. Turn the heat down and simmer gently for 5 minutes, then take off the heat to infuse for 20 minutes.

3. Meanwhile, add the rest of the sugar to the mixer, and whisk on full speed until the mixture is pale and has increased in volume (about 5 minutes). Prepare a bowl big enough for the custard, sitting within a larger bowl full of iced water.

4. Bring the milk back to a simmer, removing the vanilla pods, and pour it on to the egg mixture, beating it with a wooden spoon as you do so. Rinse out the pan thoroughly with warm water, dry, then pour the mixture back in and cook on a low heat, stirring continuously, until a line drawn in the mixture across the back of the spoon keeps its shape.

5. Pour the custard into your cold bowl and stir until it is cool enough to go into the fridge. Strain through a fine sieve into a covered container and refrigerate for at least 4 hours (it can be kept for a couple of days at this stage).

6. Stir well, then put it into the freezer for half an hour. Remove, and beat with a fork or an electric mixer until it is a uniform consistency. Repeat three times, leaving half an hour between each beating, then leave in the freezer for at least an hour, with clingfilm over the surface, before serving. Alternatively, churn in an ice cream maker and put into the freezer for an hour, with clingfilm over the top, before serving.

How to jazz up vanilla ice cream
A tub of vanilla ice cream is a very useful thing to have in the freezer – it makes even the meanest fruit salad feel like a treat, and, with a few additions, can be served as a dessert in its own right (if you have any large, robust glasses that can double as sundae glasses, all the better). Try crumbling chocolate

chip cookies or meringues on top, or soaking dried fruit briefly in booze and serving as a sort of deconstructed rum and raisin.

For the kind of popularity money can't buy, serve the ice cream with a sticky, messy, gloriously unsophisticated homemade sauce. For a hot toffee version, melt 50g of butter with 50g of light brown sugar, a pinch of salt and 3 tablespoons of golden syrup, then stir in 2 tablespoons of double cream, bring to the boil and bubble for 5 minutes until thick. To make chocolate fudge sauce, break 125g of dark chocolate into chunks and put them into a heavy-based saucepan, along with 125g of butter, 165g of light brown sugar, 1 tablespoon of golden syrup and 3 tablespoons of cold water. Heat gently, stirring to dissolve the sugar completely, then turn up the heat and bring to the boil. Allow to bubble for about 7 minutes, then stir in 1 teaspoon of vanilla extract and serve.

Perfect
Rice Pudding

A bowl of homemade rice pudding, golden and caramelized on top, warm and milky beneath, is one of the most wonderfully comforting sights on earth — it's a whole different dish to the starkly white and astonishingly bland stuff of school dinners, so often served with a mean little dollop of chewy red jam slopped carelessly into the middle.

Short-grain pudding rice is the best choice; basmati is too stodgy, and Angela Hartnett may use Arborio, but she's part Italian, which excuses her mistake — I think it makes it too chalky. It should be lubricated with a mixture of milk and cream — Marcus Wareing cooks a kind of vanilla custard for his, but I think this makes it far too rich to serve in anything but teeny-tiny restaurant portions — and baked slowly in the oven, rather than cooked on the hob as he does, or it won't develop the delicately speckled skin which connoisseurs fight over.

Although the Romans used a vaguely similar dish to treat upset stomachs, rice puddings as we know them first appeared on the scene in medieval times, when they were made with almond milk and served as a luxurious Lenten dish for the piously fasting rich, rice being a pricey import in fourteenth-century Britain. To take the rice pudding back to its roots, I've eschewed the vanilla pod used in the otherwise exemplary recipe in Simon Hopkinson and Lindsey Bareham's *The Prawn Cocktail Years*, in favour of more traditional sweet spices. Inspired by the nineteenth-century recipe recommended by Delia Smith, taken from Eliza Acton's hugely popular 1845 book *Modern Cookery for Private Families*, which stayed in print for over fifty years, I've added some syrupy sweet Pedro Ximénez sherry to give the pudding a rich raisiny edge — you can substitute brandy or dark rum if you like, or leave it out altogether if you must. Like most milk puddings, it's best left to cool for a while before serving.

Serves 4

50g butter
50g soft light brown sugar
100g pudding rice
1 litre whole milk
Zest of ½ a lemon, finely grated
1 bay leaf
½ teaspoon freshly grated nutmeg
¼ teaspoon cinnamon
A pinch of salt
150ml double cream
2 tablespoons sweet sherry,
    preferably Pedro Ximénez

1. Preheat the oven to 140°C/275°F/gas 1. Put the butter into a flameproof pie dish over a gentle heat, and, when melted, add the sugar. Stir and cook for a few minutes, then tip in the rice and stir to coat. Cook until the rice has swelled slightly (2–3 minutes), stirring continuously, then add the milk and stir

well to dislodge any clumps of rice and sugar on the bottom of the pan.

2. Add the lemon zest, bay leaf, spices and a pinch of salt, then pour in the cream and sherry and bring to a simmer.

3. Bake the pudding for about 2 hours, until it has set, but is still slightly wobbly; it may need a little longer than this, but check on it regularly. Serve warm, but not piping hot.

Perfect
Meringues

Meringues have the reputation of being difficult to make, but actually, as long as you follow a few cast-iron rules, they're a doddle. (I say that as someone who has disregarded these rules in the past, and paid the price. As with so many baking recipes, creativity with the basics will not pay off here.) Egg whites, beaten to stiff peaks, are obviously a must, plus sugar. But here things get surprisingly complicated for a dish containing just two ingredients . . .

One of the golden rules of meringue making is that all of your equipment must be scrupulously clean, without a speck of grease, or it will be much more difficult (although not impossible, as is often claimed, according to the food chemist Hervé This) to produce the desired foam with your ingredients. Marcus Wareing suggests rubbing your mixer bowl with half a lemon before beginning, to eliminate any last specks of fat before you beat the egg whites, which is an excellent idea. (Unless you're in training for Britain's Strongest Man, a food mixer or electric whisk is a must for meringue making.)

Although I've tried a few traditional recipes which whip the egg white into a foam before gradually adding the sugar, I get the best results from Yotam Ottolenghi's half Italian, half French meringue, using hot sugar – unsurprising, given that his proudly billowing creations stop pedestrian traffic outside his north London café.

Using a mix of caster and icing sugar, as Angela Nilsen of *Good Food* magazine does, makes the meringues lighter, but rather one-dimensionally sweet. If I'm making them for eating, rather than showing off, I like to use golden caster sugar – it does make them a bit beige, but the slightly caramelized flavour is gorgeous.

Meringues need clean equipment, good sugar, and, most important of all, a low oven. If you don't have an oven thermometer, and you suspect your oven is too hot, try turning it down to the coolest setting, and leaving the meringues to it. They're too good to hurry.

Makes about 10 large ones

300g caster sugar (golden if
  you prefer a more caramelized
  flavour and colour)
5 large free-range eggs, whites only, at room temperature
½ a lemon

1. Preheat the oven to 200°C/400°F/gas 6. Spread the sugar over an oven tray lined with baking parchment and cook until it has just begun to melt at the edges, but not caramelize (about 8 minutes).
2. Meanwhile, crack the eggs, being careful not to drop any yolk into your whites. If you lose any bits of shell, scoop them out with a clean spoon rather than your fingers.
3. Wipe the inside of your mixing bowl, and the whisk, with the cut side of the lemon and add the egg whites. As soon as you spot the sugar beginning to melt at the edges, set the mixer to whisk at high speed while you take the sugar out of the oven, and continue to whisk for 5 minutes.
4. The mixture should be just foamy by the time you add the sugar. Wearing oven gloves, pick up the baking parchment and tip

the hot sugar slowly into the still-whisking mixer. Continue whisking until the mixture has cooled, and is glossy and will hold its shape. Turn the oven down to its lowest setting and open the door for a few minutes to help it cool down more quickly.

5. If you want to fold through any spices or other flavourings, or roll the meringues in nuts or another topping, this is your moment – but they'll be pretty good as they are.

6. Line a baking tray with parchment, and spoon the meringue on in great gorgeous blobs – remember they'll increase in size as they dry out, so leave a good couple of centimetres between each. Put them into the oven and bake for about 3 hours, until they are crisp on the outside, and sound hollow when tapped on the bottom.

7. Turn the oven off and leave the meringues in there with the door closed for 6 hours until it has cooled completely. Then immediately transfer them to an airtight container.

How to tell if your meringues are ready to bake
Properly beaten egg white should hang from the beater in a firm tuft.
You should be able to balance an egg on top.
The egg whites should be shiny, rather than dull, and smooth, rather than grainy. If you've overbeaten them, you can rescue the situation by adding another egg white and beating until just glossy.

FACT: Baked Alaska works because meringue acts as insulation – protecting the ice cream inside from the heat.

Perfect
Pancakes

*I*t's such a shame we only make pancakes once a year in this country
– they seem to have been a bit of a favourite in the seventeenth and
eighteenth centuries, and no wonder; surviving recipes are laden
with egg yolks, cream and sweet wine. These days we tend to favour
more austere recipes to use up our eggs before the Lenten fast –
although *The Times'* Australian food writer Jill Dupleix has made a
brave stab at tradition with her rich, rum-soaked numbers. I prefer
a plainer pancake, though – all the better to anoint with lemon juice
and scatter with crunchy sugar.

While Jill and *Telegraph* rival Xanthe Clay beef
up their batter with melted butter, *Good Food*
magazine adds a dash of oil to the mix – the
butter gives a better flavour, but I think you
can achieve the same effect by cooking them
in a buttered pan instead. I do take a tip from
the two ladies and use an extra yolk, however, which gives the
pancakes a depth of flavour without that slight toughness that egg
white imparts. Allowing the batter to stand for 30 minutes, as
Hugh Fearnley-Whittingstall suggests, gives the starch a chance
to absorb water, and helps get rid of any air bubbles, which
improves their texture.

Although *Good Food* and Hugh Fearnley-Whittingstall counsel
cooking the pancakes over a moderate heat, I prefer to follow

Professor Peter Barham, physicist and adviser to Heston Blumenthal, in getting the pan really hot, because I like mine thin and crisp – you can turn it down before cooking if you prefer a softer finish. Spread the batter as thin as possible for delicately lacy edges – and treat the first pancake as an experiment; it usually goes wrong, which is a good excuse to treat it as a cook's perk.

These are also good wrapped around a creamy seafood filling, stuffed with spinach and ricotta and gratinated – or slathered with chopped banana and chocolate sauce. Versatile, eh?

Makes about 8

125g plain flour
A pinch of salt
1 large free-range egg,
   plus 1 large egg yolk
225ml whole or semi-skimmed milk
30g butter, softened

1. Sift the flour into a large mixing bowl and add a pinch of salt. Make a well in the centre, and pour the egg and the yolk into it. Mix the milk with 2 tablespoons of cold water and pour a little in with the egg.
2. Use a balloon whisk to whisk the flour into the liquid ingredients, drawing it gradually into the middle until you have a smooth paste the consistency of double cream. Whisk the rest of the milk in until the batter has more of the consistency of single cream. Cover and refrigerate for at least 30 minutes.
3. Heat the butter in a crêpe pan or a 20cm non-stick frying pan

on a medium-high heat — you only need enough fat to just grease the bottom of the pan. It should be hot enough that the batter sizzles when it hits it.

4. Spread a small ladleful of batter across the bottom of the pan, quickly swirling to coat. Tip any excess away. When it begins to set, loosen the edges with a thin spatula or palette knife, and when it begins to colour on the bottom, flip it over with the same instrument and cook for another 30 seconds. (If you're feeling cocky, you can also toss the pancake after loosening it: grasp the handle firmly with both hands, then jerk the pan up and slightly towards you.)

5. Pancakes are best eaten as soon as possible, before they go rubbery, but if you're cooking for a crowd, keep them separate until you're ready to serve by layering them up between pieces of kitchen roll.

Perfect
Fruit Salad

My heart always sank when my mum brought fruit salad out for
pudding – particularly once it had been round the table and all that
was left were a few browning bits of apple and a mushy slice of
banana. It was the kind of dessert that could make even a pot of
yoghurt look pretty decadent. A fruit salad is, by its very nature,
simple – so you've got nothing to hide behind. Either do it well, or
serve some fresh fruit instead.

Obviously your recipe is going to depend on the season (there's no
point buying strawberries in February, or apples in June, they just
won't taste as good) and the occasion, but do try and theme your
salad rather than simply chopping up a medley of the usual suspects
and sticking them in a bowl together. There's little use pushing the
boat out with a mango (although good call – a mean fruit salad is a
sad sight indeed) and then pairing it with a very British russet apple
or some woodland berries: it's like expecting parsnips to go well with
pak choi. Tropical, autumn, summer pudding – pick three or
four fruits, and do them really well – add any bananas just
before serving, so they don't go mushy. In the
winter, soak some dried figs or prunes in
juice (or booze) and mix with Christmassy
clementines or baked apples instead.

Dousing the salad with orange juice is a good way to keep flavours
fresh, but if you're making a salad for guests, make an effort with

your own syrup – I've given an example below, but it's easy to put any fruit or flavouring you like in. Jamie Oliver does a lovely mint one, Gino D'Acampo has a recipe for *macedonio di frutta* in which he soaks his fruit in amaretto before serving, and Delia goes a bit wild with spices and rum in her planter's punch tropical fruit salad.

Put the finishing touches to your fruit salad with a few passion fruit seeds, cinnamon sticks or sprigs of mint, and serve it with something suitably sumptuous, be it Greek yoghurt or some fresh young goat's cheese and a drizzle of honey. Properly prepared, fruit salad can be a real treat – especially with a generous scoop of homemade ice cream (see page 230).

For the passion fruit syrup

Makes 200ml

6 ripe passion fruit – it's a good
   idea to buy them a few days
   ahead and allow them to ripen
   at home, until the skins are
   wrinkled and deep purple in colour
50g caster sugar
Zest of 1 lime, finely grated

1. Put the sugar into a small pan with 75ml water and bring to the boil. Meanwhile, cut the passion fruit in half and scoop out the pulp.
2. Reduce the heat and simmer the syrup for a few minutes until slightly thickened, then turn it off, stir in the pulp and lime zest, allow to cool and then refrigerate for a few hours before stirring into the fruit salad.

Bibliography

I've long had a weakness for cookbooks — this book was inspired by the embarrassment of choice when it came to making, say, a minestrone, but it's also proved a superb excuse to abandon all pretence of a healthy interest in the things and go utterly wild. My collection has mushroomed alarmingly as a result. This is not an exhaustive list of every title I've consulted in the course of my (painstaking) research, but it includes the ones I've found the most consistently useful, so, should your curiosity be piqued by any of the recipes mentioned, you can follow them up.

For anyone beginning to build their own cookery library, I'd advise investing in a comprehensive bible-style book, such as those published by the Leiths or Ballymaloe Cookery Schools or, of  course, Delia Smith, an everyday cookbook (Nigel Slater's *Real Food* is an excellent example, and I also use Diana Henry's *Cook Simple* an awful lot), plus a few more specialist ones — fish, French food, frying; whatever you're particularly interested in. Local libraries are also a great source of cookery books, as long as you're able to resist the temptation to keep them within splattering distance of the action.

I also use the internet a lot for cooking, primarily because it's an excellent source of recipes that have been published in newspapers and magazines (Skye Gyngell in the *Independent*, Xanthe Clay in the *Telegraph*, Hugh Fearnley-Whittingstall, Yotam Ottolenghi, Dan Lepard – and many more – in the *Guardian*), but also because I am lazy, and it's quicker to type in 'Jamie Oliver fish pie' than it is to go and hunt through his many cookbooks to find a recipe. (Try not to use your laptop with doughy fingers, however; it can be expensive.) For this reason, I've also included a list of websites I use regularly.

Aikens, Tom, *Fish* (Ebury, 2008)

Allen, Darina, *Darina Allen's Ballymaloe Cookery Course* (Kyle Cathie, 2007)

Allen, Rachel, *Bake* (Collins, 2008)

Bareham, Lindsey, *A Celebration of Soup* (Penguin, 2001)

Bareham, Lindsey, and Hopkinson, Simon, *The Prawn Cocktail Years* (Michael Joseph, 2006)

Bayless, Rick, *Mexican Kitchen* (Absolute Press, 2007)

Beeton, Isabella, *Mrs Beeton's Book of Household Management* (Oxford University Press, 2000)

Bertinet, Richard, *Dough: Simple Contemporary Bread* (Kyle Cathie, 2008)

Blanc, Raymond, *Foolproof French Cookery* (BBC Books, 2002)

Blumenthal, Heston, *In Search of Total Perfection* (Bloomsbury, 2009)

Boggiano, Angela, *Pie* (Mitchell Beazley, 2009)

Burrell, Fiona, *Leiths Baking Bible* (Bloomsbury, 2006)

Campion, Charles, *Food from Fire: The Real Barbecue Book* (Mitchell Beazley, 2006)

Child, Julia, Bertholle, Louisette, and Beck, Simone, *Mastering the Art of French Cooking* (Penguin, 2009)

Clark, Max, and Spaull, Susan, *Leiths Meat Bible* (Bloomsbury, 2010)

Costa, Margaret, *Four Seasons Cookery Book* (Grub Street, 2008)

David, Elizabeth, *A Book of Mediterranean Food* (Penguin, 1998)

David, Elizabeth, *French Provincial Cooking* (Grub Street, 2007)

David, Elizabeth, *Italian Food* (Penguin, 1998)

Davidson, Alan, ed., *The Oxford Companion to Food* (Oxford University Press, 1999)

Deighton, Len, *Len Deighton's French Cooking for Men* (HarperCollins, 2010)

Del Conte, Anna, *Risotto with Nettles* (Vintage, 2010)

Dixon-Wright, Clarissa, *Clarissa's Comfort Food* (Kyle Cathie, 2008)

Fearnley-Whittingstall, Hugh, *The River Cottage Meat Book* (Hodder & Stoughton, 2004)

Fearnley-Whittingstall, Hugh, and Fisher, Nick, *The River Cottage Fish Book* (Bloomsbury, 2007)

Fisher, M. F. K., *An Alphabet for Gourmets* (North Point Press, 1989)

Gedda, Gui, and Moines, Marie-Pierre, *Cooking School Provence: Cook, Shop and Eat Like a Local* (Dorling Kindersley, 2007)

Good Housekeeping Cookery Book: The Cook's Classic Companion (Collins & Brown, 2004)

Gray, Rose, and Rogers, Ruth, *The River Café Classic Italian Cookbook* (Michael Joseph, 2009)

Grigson, Jane, *English Food* (Penguin, 1998)

Grigson, Jane, *Jane Grigson's Vegetable Book* (Penguin, 1998)

Hartnett, Angela, *Angela Hartnett's Cucina: Three Generations of Italian Family Cooking* (Ebury Press, 2007)

Hilferty, Trish, *Lobster & Chips* (Absolute Press, 2005)

Hopkinson, Simon, and Bareham, Lindsey, *Roast Chicken and Other Stories* (Ebury Press, 1999)

Jackson, C. J., and Waldegrave, Caroline, *Leiths Fish Bible* (Bloomsbury, 2005)

Jaffrey, Madhur, *Madhur Jaffrey's Ultimate Curry Bible* (Ebury, 2003)

Keller, Thomas, *Bouchon* (Artisan Division of Workman Publishing, 2004)

King, Si, and Myers, Dave, *The Hairy Bikers' Food Tour of Britain* (W&N, 2009)

Larousse Gastronomique (Hamlyn, 2009)

Lawson, Nigella, *How to be a Domestic Goddess* (Chatto & Windus, 2003)

Lawson, Nigella, *How to Eat: The Pleasures and Principles of Good Food* (Chatto & Windus, 1999)

Leith, Prue, and Waldegrave, Caroline, *Leiths Cookery Bible* (Bloomsbury, 2003)

Lepard, Dan, *The Handmade Loaf* (Mitchell Beazley, 2008)

Locatelli, Giorgio, *Made in Italy* (Fourth Estate, 2008)

McGee, Harold, *McGee on Food and Cooking* (Hodder & Stoughton, 2004)

Miers, Thomasina, *Mexican Food Made Simple* (Hodder & Stoughton, 2010)

Nilsen, Angela, *Good Food: The Ultimate Recipe Book* (BBC Books, 2007)

Norrington-Davies, Tom, *Just Like Mother Used to Make* (Cassell Illustrated, 2004)

Norwak, Mary, *English Puddings Sweet & Savoury* (Grub Street, 2009)

Oliver, Jamie, *Jamie's Dinners* (Penguin, 2004)

Oliver, Jamie, *Jamie's Italy* (Penguin, 2005)

Owen, Sri, *The Rice Book* (Frances Lincoln, 2003)

Paston-Williams, Sara, *Good Old-Fashioned Puddings* (National Trust Books, 2007)

Pettigrew, Jane, *Traditional Teatime Recipes* (National Trust Books, 2007)

Powell, Julie, *Cleaving* (Fig Tree, 2009)

Prince, Rose, *The New English Kitchen* (Fourth Estate, 2005)

Richards, Morfudd, *Lola's Ice Creams and Sundaes* (Ebury, 2009)

Roux, Michel, *Sauces: Savoury & Sweet* (Quadrille, 2009)

Roux, Michel, *Michel Roux: A Life in the Kitchen* (W&N, 2009)

Sampson, Susan, *12,167 Kitchen and Cooking Secrets* (Robert Rose, 2009)

Segnit, Niki, *The Flavour Thesaurus* (Bloomsbury, 2010)

Slater, Nigel, *Real Fast Puddings* (Penguin, 2006)

Slater, Nigel, *Real Food* (Fourth Estate, 2009)

Smith, Delia, *Complete Cookery Course* (BBC Books, 1992)

Stevens, Daniel, *Bread: River Cottage Handbook No.3* (Bloomsbury, 2009)

Tamimi, Sami, and Ottolenghi, Yotam, *Ottolenghi: The Cookbook* (Ebury, 2008)

The Silver Spoon (Phaidon, 2005)

This, Hervé, *Kitchen Mysteries: Revealing the Science of Cooking* (Columbia University Press, 2007)

Torode, John, *John Torode's Beef* (Quadrille, 2008)

Wareing, Marcus, *How to Cook the Perfect . . .* (Dorling Kindersley, 2007)

Websites

bbcgoodfood.com

chowhound.chow.com

cooksillustrated.com

deliaonline.com

deliciousmagazine.co.uk

egullet.org

gastronomydomine.com

jamieoliver.com

nigella.com

seriouseats.com

The food sections of many newspaper websites (including the *New York Times*, although you'll have to convert the measurements using something like onlineconversion.com) are also an invaluable source of recipes and inspiration.

Acknowledgements

Thanks to Amy, Nicole, Rick and especially Susan at the *Guardian* for having faith in me in the first place, Juliet and Jenny at Fig Tree for pursuing me with such dedication — and, along with Ellie, Annie and all my proofreaders and recipe testers, for doing such a great job with this book — and Sarah and Lara at United Agents for keeping me sane. I also owe an enormous debt of gratitude to the many very talented chefs and food writers who have so good-naturedly allowed me to pull apart their recipes week after week in pursuit of perfection.

I am also grateful to my family and friends, particularly my parents, Alex, Ali, Anna and Emma, for their devotion to critiquing crackling and assessing pesto, and for allowing me to hijack endless dinner parties with my notebook. And, of course, thanks to my *Guardian* readers, without whose advice and encouragement this book would have been very much the poorer.

Index

(Perfect recipes in bold)